PLAY LIKE A
GIRL

A graphic memoir

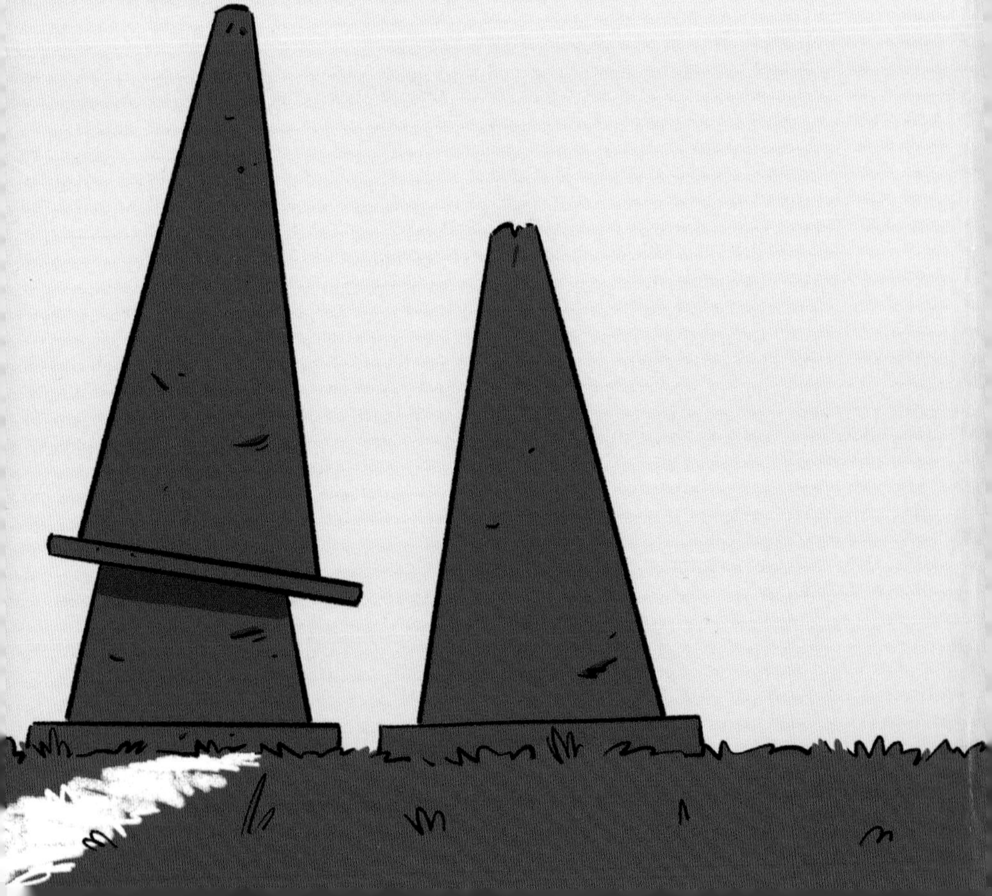

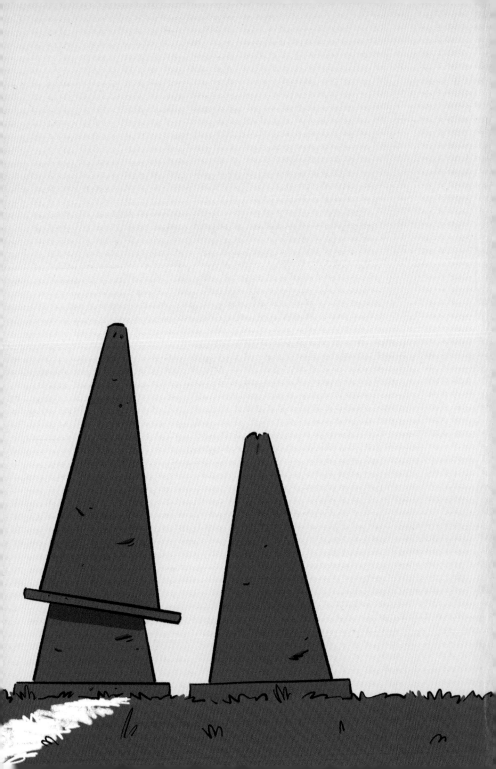

MISTY WILSON

PLAY LIKE A
GIRL

A graphic memoir

ILLUSTRATED BY
DAVID WILSON

BALZER + BRAY
IMPRINTS OF HARPERCOLLINS PUBLISHERS

HARPER
alley

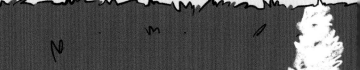

Balzer + Bray is an imprint of HarperCollins Publishers.

HarperAlley is an imprint of HarperCollins Publishers.

Play Like a Girl

Text copyright © 2022 by Misty Wilson

Illustrations copyright © 2022 by David Wilson

www.harperalley.com

Library of Congress Control Number: 2022931778

ISBN 978-0-06-306469-0 (trade bdg.) — ISBN 978-0-06-306468-3 (pbk.)

Typography by David Wilson and Dana Fritts

22 23 24 25 26 RTLO 10 9 8 7 6 5 4 3 2 1

First Edition

FOR ANYONE STRUGGLING TO
FIND THEIR PLACE.
BE UNAPOLOGETICALLY YOU.

CHAPTER 1

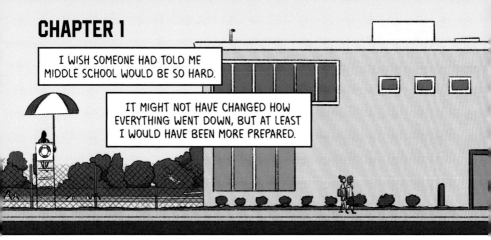

I WISH SOMEONE HAD TOLD ME MIDDLE SCHOOL WOULD BE SO HARD.

IT MIGHT NOT HAVE CHANGED HOW EVERYTHING WENT DOWN, BUT AT LEAST I WOULD HAVE BEEN MORE PREPARED.

IT ALL STARTED THE SUMMER BEFORE SEVENTH GRADE...

BREE, LOOK! FOOTBALL!

LET'S GO WATCH!

BUT I JUST WANT TO GO SWIMMING.

COME ON! WE GO SWIMMING ALMOST EVERY DAY.

THIS IS THE FIRST TIME I'VE SEEN THE BOYS PLAY FOOTBALL HERE ALL SUMMER!

UGH...

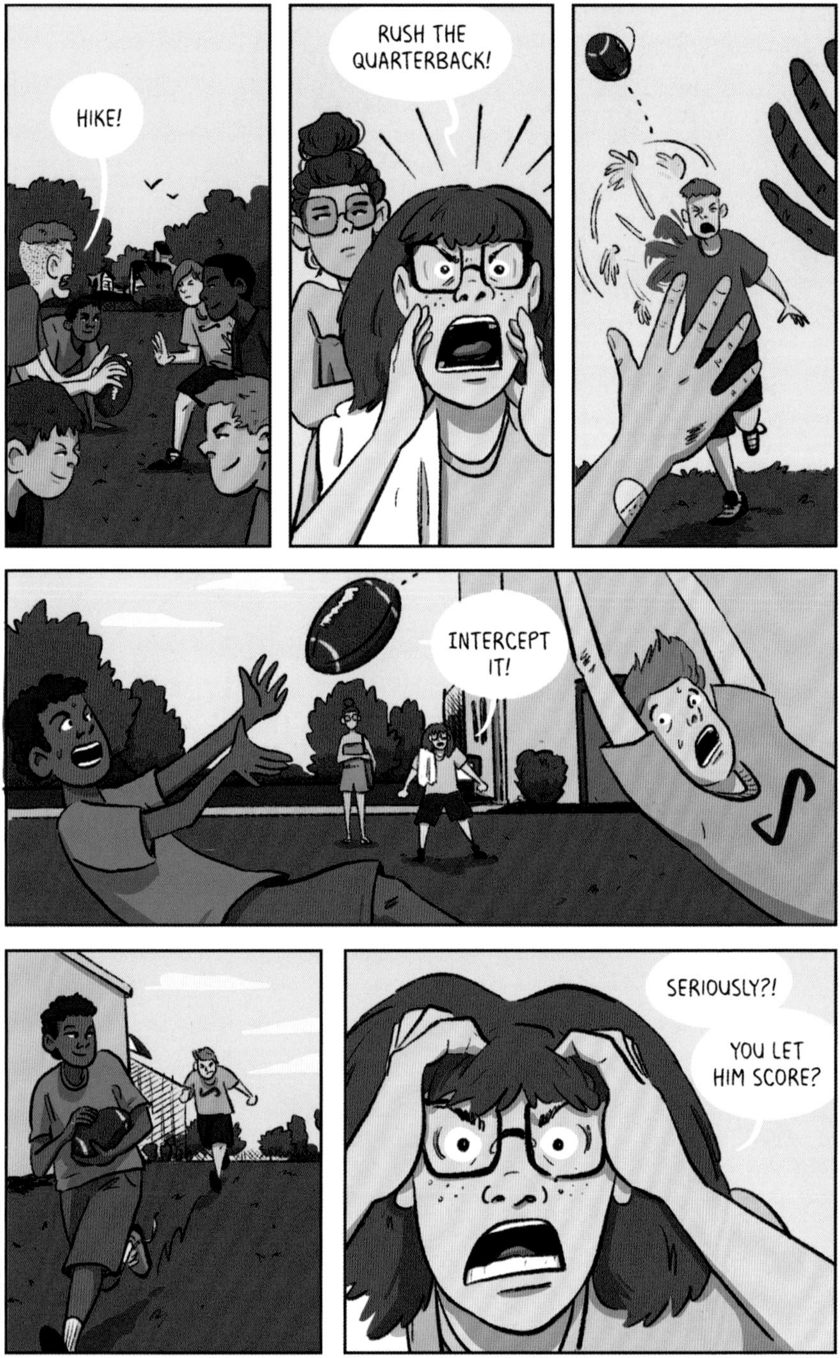
HIKE!
RUSH THE QUARTERBACK!
INTERCEPT IT!
SERIOUSLY?!
YOU LET HIM SCORE?

WOW.

WHAT?

YOU'RE STARTING TO SOUND LIKE MY DAD.

IT'S JUST FOOTBALL.

JUST FOOTBALL?!

ARE YOU KIDDING ME?

IT'S THE BEST SPORT!

IT HAS STRATEGY, TEAMWORK, AND BEST OF ALL, YOU GET TO **TACKLE**!

IN OTHER SPORTS, I GET IN TROUBLE FOR BARELY TOUCHING PEOPLE!

ALL RIGHT. CALM DOWN. I GET IT. YOU LIKE RUNNING AROUND HITTING PEOPLE.

RELAXING IN THE SUN IS MORE MY STYLE.

CAN WE PLEASE GO TO THE POOL NOW?

YOU GO AHEAD.

I'LL MEET YOU THERE.

BREE AND I WERE BEST FRIENDS, AND WE DID ALMOST EVERYTHING TOGETHER...

...EXCEPT WHEN I WAS COMPETING AGAINST THE BOYS.

ZOOM!

SLAM!

IS THAT ALL YOU GOT?

YEAH, I'M DONE.

HUFF...

HEY, GUYS! CAN I PLAY?

I DON'T THINK SO.

DON'T YOU HAVE FRIENDS YOU CAN GO HANG OUT WITH OR SOMETHING?

UM, YOU GUYS **ARE** MY FRIENDS, NICK.

WHY CAN'T I PLAY?

WE SIGNED UP FOR THE TOWN'S FOOTBALL LEAGUE. THE SEASON STARTS NEXT WEEK, SO WE JUST WANT TO PRACTICE AS A TEAM.

BESIDES, FOOTBALL REALLY ISN'T A SPORT FOR **GIRLS**.

HOW COME THEY WERE ALL STANDING THERE, ACTING LIKE THEY AGREED WITH COLE?

WHAT?!

THEY WERE SUPPOSED TO BE MY FRIENDS...

...YET NOT A SINGLE ONE OF THEM WAS STICKING UP FOR ME.

YOU CAN'T BE SERIOUS!

I'M STRONGER AND FASTER THAN ALL OF YOU! AND YOU KNOW IT!

I'VE BEEN KICKING YOUR BUTTS SINCE KINDERGARTEN, INCLUDING WHEN WE'VE PLAYED FOOTBALL.

THAT WAS ON THE PLAYGROUND, MISTY. THIS IS DIFFERENT. WE'RE PRACTICING FOR THE REAL THING.

SORRY.

WHATEVER.

THERE WAS NO WAY THE BOYS WERE GONNA KEEP ME ON THE SIDELINES.

IF THEY COULD PLAY FOOTBALL, THEN SO COULD I.

HIKE!

I WAS JUST GONNA HAVE TO SIGN UP, TOO.

YOUTH FOOTBALL

SIGN-UPS JULY 8-15

FUNDRAISER TUE

I COULDN'T WAIT TO TELL BREE MY PLAN.

MAYBE I COULD CONVINCE HER TO PLAY WITH ME.

WAIT... ...IS BREE TALKING TO... ...AVA?

AVA WAS ON THE BASKETBALL TEAM WITH ME. SHE WAS POPULAR, ATHLETIC, PRETTY, WITH PERFECT BLOND HAIR—THAT WASN'T POOFY LIKE MINE—AND EVERYONE SEEMED TO LIKE HER, ESPECIALLY THE BOYS...

...WHICH IS PROBABLY WHY I FELT SO AWKWARD AROUND HER. SHE WAS THE **DEFINITION OF COOL**, AND I WAS, WELL, **THE OPPOSITE**.

WE HARDLY EVER TALKED, EVEN AT BASKETBALL PRACTICE.

HEY, BREE!

HEY, AVA!

DON'T GET ME WRONG. I **TRIED** TO TALK TO HER, BUT SHE ALWAYS GAVE ME THIS LOOK, LIKE I WAS FROM OUTER SPACE OR SOMETHING.

The Look

HI...

WAZZUP?!

NOT MUCH...

DO YOU THINK YOU USED ENOUGH SUNSCREEN?

AT LEAST IT HIDES ALL THOSE FRECKLES.

I COULDN'T BELIEVE BREE SAID THAT IN FRONT OF AVA, BUT I DID WHAT I ALWAYS DID WHEN I FELT UNCOMFORTABLE...

...I LAUGHED ALONG WITH THEM.

I JUST HOPED THE SUNSCREEN ALSO HID HOW MORTIFIED I WAS.

ANYWAY, I'M ACTUALLY SUPPOSED TO BE HELPING MY MOM WATCH MY LITTLE SISTER, SO I'M GOING TO HEAD BACK OVER.

SEE YA, BREE.

SEE YA!

BYE.

SINCE WHEN DO YOU TALK TO AVA?!

WE BUNKED TOGETHER AT THAT RIDICULOUS CAMP MY DAD MADE ME GO TO.

SHE WANTS TO START HANGING OUT.

WAIT... REALLY?

SO YOU TWO ARE LIKE ACTUAL FRIENDS NOW...

YEAH, I GUESS WE ARE.

IF **BREE** COULD BE FRIENDS WITH AVA, I COULD BE, TOO. IT'S NOT LIKE BREE WAS EXACTLY COOL.

AVA JUST NEEDED TO GET TO KNOW ME BETTER. AND NOW THAT SHE WAS FRIENDS WITH MY BEST FRIEND, THAT COULD DEFINITELY HAPPEN.

HECK YEAH! SEVENTH GRADE IS GONNA BE AWESOME!

OH, BY THE WAY...

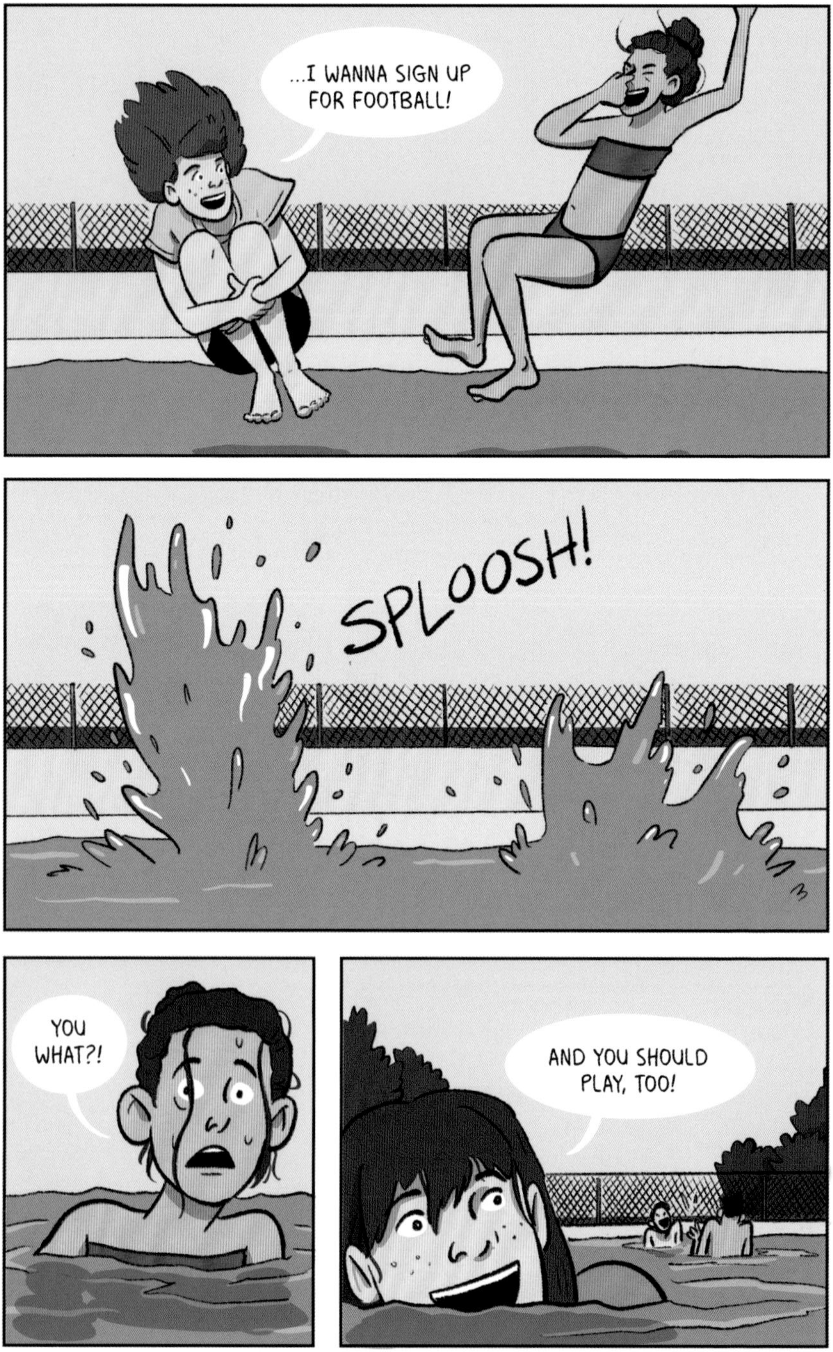
...I WANNA SIGN UP FOR FOOTBALL!
SPLOOSH!
YOU WHAT?!
AND YOU SHOULD PLAY, TOO!

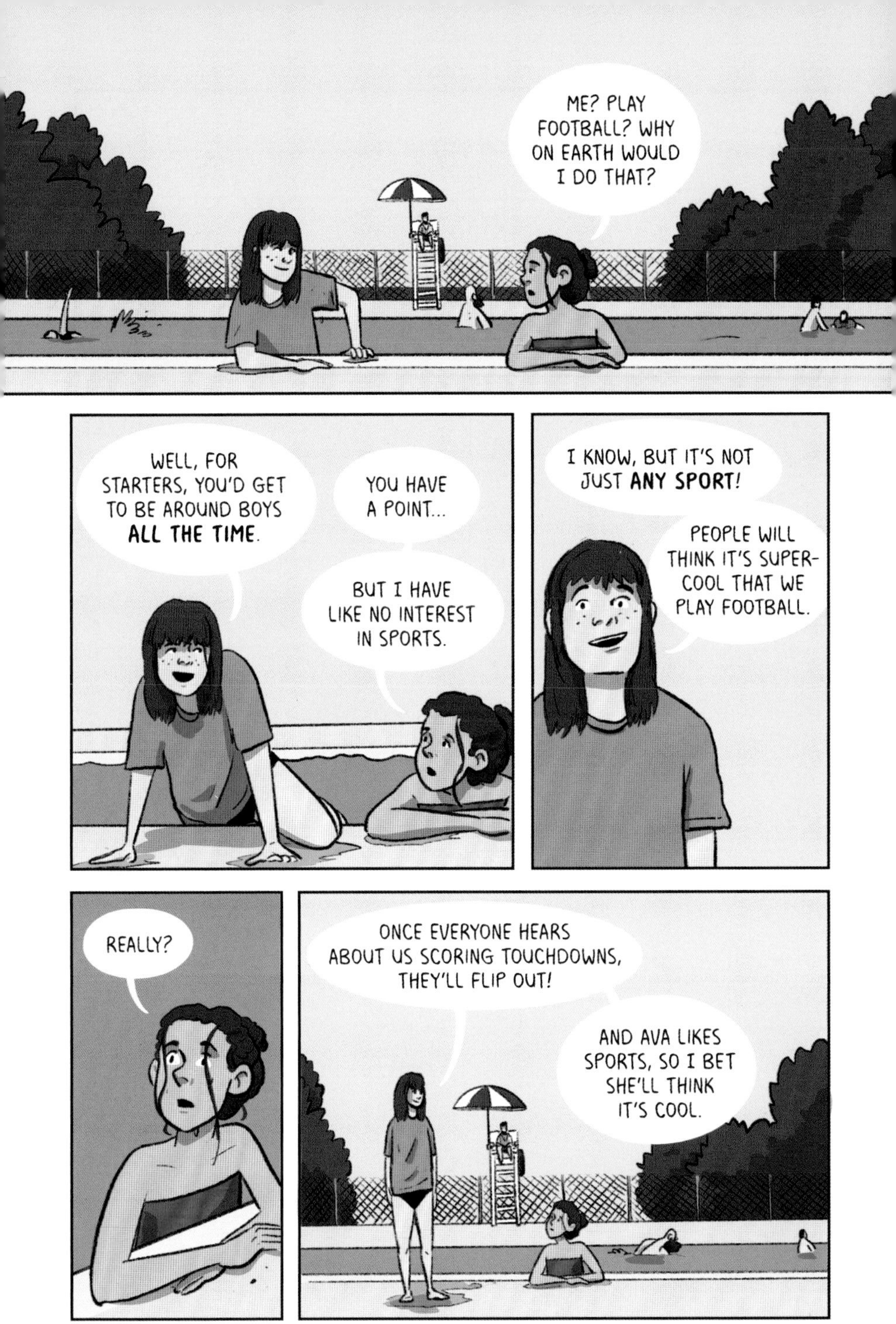
ME? PLAY FOOTBALL? WHY ON EARTH WOULD I DO THAT?
WELL, FOR STARTERS, YOU'D GET TO BE AROUND BOYS **ALL THE TIME**.
YOU HAVE A POINT...
BUT I HAVE LIKE NO INTEREST IN SPORTS.
I KNOW, BUT IT'S NOT JUST **ANY SPORT**!
PEOPLE WILL THINK IT'S SUPER-COOL THAT WE PLAY FOOTBALL.
REALLY?
ONCE EVERYONE HEARS ABOUT US SCORING TOUCHDOWNS, THEY'LL FLIP OUT!
AND AVA LIKES SPORTS, SO I BET SHE'LL THINK IT'S COOL.

ALSO, YOU'D BE PLAYING WITH YOUR BEST FRIEND IN THE WHOLE WORLD, WHO COULD TEACH YOU EVERYTHING YOU NEED TO KNOW.

AND I **PROMISE** IT'LL BE FUN!

OKAY, OKAY, I'LL PLAY.

SERIOUSLY?

YEAH, YOU HAD ME AT **BOYS**.

HA!

AHH! WE'RE PLAYING FOOTBALL!

WHAT AM I GETTING MYSELF INTO?

IT'S GONNA BE AMAZING!

HOP!

NO RUNNING!

NOW I JUST HAD TO ASK MY PARENTS, AND THEY'D TOTALLY BE OKAY WITH IT...

...AT LEAST, I HOPED...

DINNERS AT MY HOUSE WERE **CHAOTIC**.

BUT I KIND OF HOPED THAT MEANT MY MOM AND MY STEPDAD, CRAIG, WOULD BE TOO DISTRACTED TO THINK TOO MUCH ABOUT ME BEING **TACKLED**, AND THEY'D JUST SAY YES.

MOM, CAN I GO TO TYLER'S HOUSE THIS WEEKEND?

NO, BARBIE, THIS IS MY FOOD!

OPEN UP!

MORE!

THAT'S FINE, DEREK.

LIV, NO BARBIES AT THE TABLE.

IT'S GOING TO BE ANOTHER HOT ONE TOMORROW.

THE PL[AY]

YEAH, BARBIES ARE FOR BABIES!

MOM! DEREK CALLED ME A BABY!

DEREK, STOP PICKING ON YOUR SISTER!

MOM, DO YOU THINK MAYBE I CAN PLAY FOOTBALL...?

BITE!

OW!

INSTEAD, THEY WERE TOO DISTRACTED TO EVEN LISTEN TO ME.

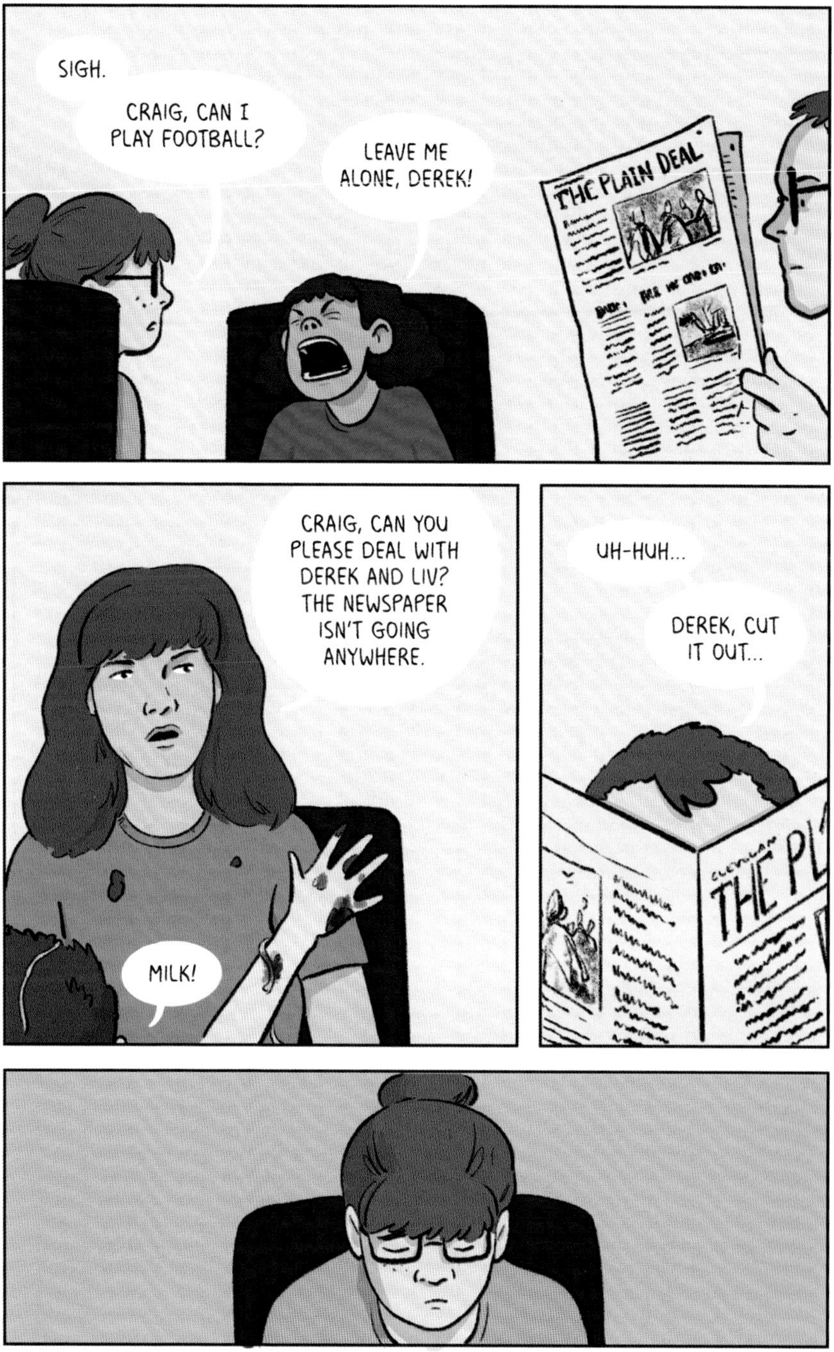
SIGH.
CRAIG, CAN I PLAY FOOTBALL?
LEAVE ME ALONE, DEREK!
THE PLAIN DEAL
CRAIG, CAN YOU PLEASE DEAL WITH DEREK AND LIV? THE NEWSPAPER ISN'T GOING ANYWHERE.
MILK!
UH-HUH...
DEREK, CUT IT OUT...
THE PL

MOM!

CRAIG!

ANSWER MEEEEE!

PLEASE.

WHAT?

I WANT TO PLAY FOOTBALL!

LIKE POWDER PUFF?

LIKE FLAG FOOTBALL?

NO.

REAL FOOTBALL.

TACKLE FOOTBALL.

WITH THE BOYS.

CAN I?

PLEASE?

JUDGING BY HOW THEY WERE LOOKING AT ME, THERE WAS NO WAY THEY WERE GONNA SAY YES.

HA-HA-HA!

YOU?!

PLAY FOOTBALL?

DEREK! STOP IT!

THE IDEA OF ME PLAYING FOOTBALL WASN'T **THAT** BANANAS. I WAS SO SICK OF BOYS ACTING LIKE I COULDN'T DO IT.

MISTY, I DON'T KNOW...

...IT COULD BE DANGEROUS.

I'M NOT SURE IT'S A GOOD IDEA.

CRAIG, WHAT DO YOU THINK?

WELL, NOW WOULD BE A GOOD TIME FOR IT...

THE BOYS ARE ONLY GOING TO GET BIGGER...

I THINK IT'S A FANTASTIC IDEA, BUT I'LL LEAVE IT UP TO YOU.

SUMMER WAS ALSO SUPPOSED TO BE OUR BREAK FROM SPORTS. ALL YOU KIDS ARE HOME NOW...

...AND I DON'T KNOW IF WE HAVE TIME TO TAKE YOU TO PRACTICES.

I'LL WALK IF I HAVE TO! I DON'T CARE!

I WAS DESPERATE. PLUS, DEREK'S REACTION HAD CONVINCED ME THAT I **HAD** TO PLAY.

I THINK WE COULD FIGURE IT OUT...

THE PLAIN

SIGH.

ALL RIGHT. I GUESS YOU CAN PLAY.

I JUST DON'T WANT YOU TO GET HURT.

AND REMEMBER, IT'S OKAY IF IT ENDS UP BEING TOO HARD. THERE'S NO SHAME IN QUITTING.

THANKS, MOM!

I GUESS I WAS ALSO GONNA HAVE TO SHOW MOM I COULD DO THIS.

YES! FRIDAY NIGHTS UNDER THE LIGHTS! I CAN'T WAIT!

THE PLAI

I COULDN'T BELIEVE IT. I WAS ACTUALLY GONNA BE ON A REAL FOOTBALL TEAM!

CHAPTER 2

FIRST FOOTBALL PRACTICE.

I'M SO EXCITED!

THE BOYS HAVE BEEN HERE FOR A WHILE WARMING UP. I'LL HAVE TO START GETTING HERE EARLY, TOO.

SERIOUSLY?

TO PRACTICE **BEFORE** PRACTICE?

IF IT'S WHAT THE BOYS DO, THEN YEAH.

WELCOME, LADIES! I'M GEORGE, BUT YOU CAN CALL ME COACH G. AND THIS IS COACH DAVE, OUR ASSISTANT COACH.

YOU TWO
READY TO
SWEAT?

YES!

SURE...

GREAT! JOIN THE REST
OF THE TEAM, AND WE'LL
GET STARTED SOON.

I COULDN'T WAIT TO
SURPRISE THE BOYS.

25

HI, EVERYONE!

WHAT ARE **YOU** DOING HERE?

BEFORE LAST WEEK, COLE HAD NEVER BEEN THIS MEAN. HE WAS MY TOUGHEST COMPETITION, BUT WE'D ALWAYS GOTTEN ALONG.

NOW IT SEEMED LIKE HE HATED ME JUST FOR BEING ON HIS TURF.

THE SAME THING AS YOU—PLAYING FOOTBALL. OBVIOUSLY!

UGH.

YOU CAN'T BE SERIOUS.

SO MUCH FOR HAVING A CHANCE AT A WINNING SEASON.

DON'T WORRY. THEY WON'T LAST LONG.

IGNORE THEM.

I JUST DON'T GET WHY THEY'RE BEING SUCH JERKS.

I THINK SOME OF THE GUYS ARE JUST AFRAID WE'LL LOSE GAMES IF WE HAVE GIRLS ON THE TEAM.

LET ME GET THIS STRAIGHT.

WE'RE ALL "FRIENDS" UNTIL THEY THINK I'M GONNA MAKE THEM LOSE? THAT'S MESSED UP!

I BARELY KNEW CHARLIE. HE WAS A QUIET KID FROM SCHOOL WHO DIDN'T PLAY WITH US AT RECESS. SO I DIDN'T MEAN TO BLOW UP ON HIM—I WAS JUST SO STINKIN' MAD.

NEWS FLASH!

I'M NOT HERE TO LOSE!

IN FACT, I'M READY TO GET OUR PADS AND CRUSH COLE.

OH.

WELL, WE DON'T START TACKLING FOR ANOTHER TWO WEEKS...

WHA??

YEAH, WE HAVE CONDITIONING.

LOTS OF RUNNING, PUSH-UPS, SIT-UPS, AGILITY DRILLS, AND THEN MORE RUNNING.

IT'S PRETTY TERRIBLE.

ALL RIGHT, BEARS! WARM-UP TIME! FIVE LAPS! LET'S GET MOVING!

LAPS? I COULD DO THAT. I WAS AN AWESOME RUNNER!

WOO-HOO! GO, MISTY!

GREAT. YOU GOT SLOW THIS SUMMER, TOO.

HE DID **NOT** JUST CALL ME SLOW.

I CAN OUTRUN THIS TURD ANY DAY OF THE WEEK!

VROOOOM

HEH.

TWO SECONDS LATER.

WHEW!

FIGURES.

I GUESS I **WAS** KIND OF OUT OF SHAPE AFTER DOING ABSOLUTELY NOTHING BUT LOUNGING BY THE POOL ALL SUMMER...

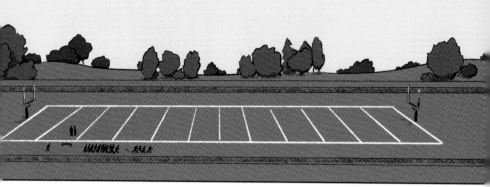

SIT-UPS!
LET'S GO!

SURE, I WAS TIRED. BUT I KNEW I COULD DO SIT-UPS. IN PE, I'D ALWAYS DONE MORE THAN EVERYONE IN MY CLASS!

ABS
OF STEEL,
BABY!

PUNCH

TWENTY!

IT BURNS!

JUST WHEN I THOUGHT PRACTICE COULDN'T POSSIBLY GET ANY WORSE...

...IT GOT EVEN HOTTER...

...AND I COULD FEEL MYSELF GETTING SUNBURNT.

IT WAS **MISERABLE**.

SO HOT.

SO THIRSTY.

I THINK I'M GOING TO DIE.

MIGHT PUKE.

STOP CHATTING, LADIES, OR YOU'LL BE RUNNING MORE LAPS.

HA!

GRRR...

APPROXIMATELY ONE MILLION YEARS LATER.

OKAY, EVERYBODY, GRAB SOME WATER!

THERE WASN'T ENOUGH WATER ON THE PLANET FOR HOW THIRSTY I WAS...

TIME FOR PUSH-UPS! LET'S GO!

HUFF

HUFF

HUFF

AND THE BREAK WAS **WAY** TOO SHORT...

ONE!

WHAT THE HECK?

PATHETIC.

SHUT UP, MAX. **YOU'RE** PATHETIC.

PUSH-UPS WERE HARD, BUT WAS BREE REALLY GIVING UP AFTER ONLY ONE?!

I'D KNOWN MAX SINCE HE MOVED HERE IN SECOND GRADE. WE WEREN'T REALLY FRIENDS BECAUSE HE WAS ALWAYS SUCH A MEAN LITTLE TWERP...

...BUT THIS TIME, HE WASN'T WRONG.

BREE WASN'T EVEN **TRYING!**

NOT GONNA LIE, I WAS PRETTY IRRITATED.

BUT CRAIG WAS CHEERING ME ON...

MISTY! YOU'VE GOT THIS! KEEP GOING!

THIRTEEN!

HA! YEAH, MISTY, KEEP GOING.

...AND EVEN THOUGH IT WAS A LITTLE EMBARRASSING...

...IT WAS BASICALLY THE ONLY THING KEEPING ME FROM COLLAPSING... AT LEAST FOR A LITTLE WHILE.

BUT I WAS LOSING STAMINA...

THAT'S IT FOR TODAY! CIRCLE UP!

FINALLY!

LIKE I SAID...

...PATHETIC.

I WAS TOO TIRED TO CARE ABOUT THE BOYS TALKING SMACK.

BESIDES, SOME OF THEM HAD STRUGGLED TODAY, TOO. SO, WHATEVER.

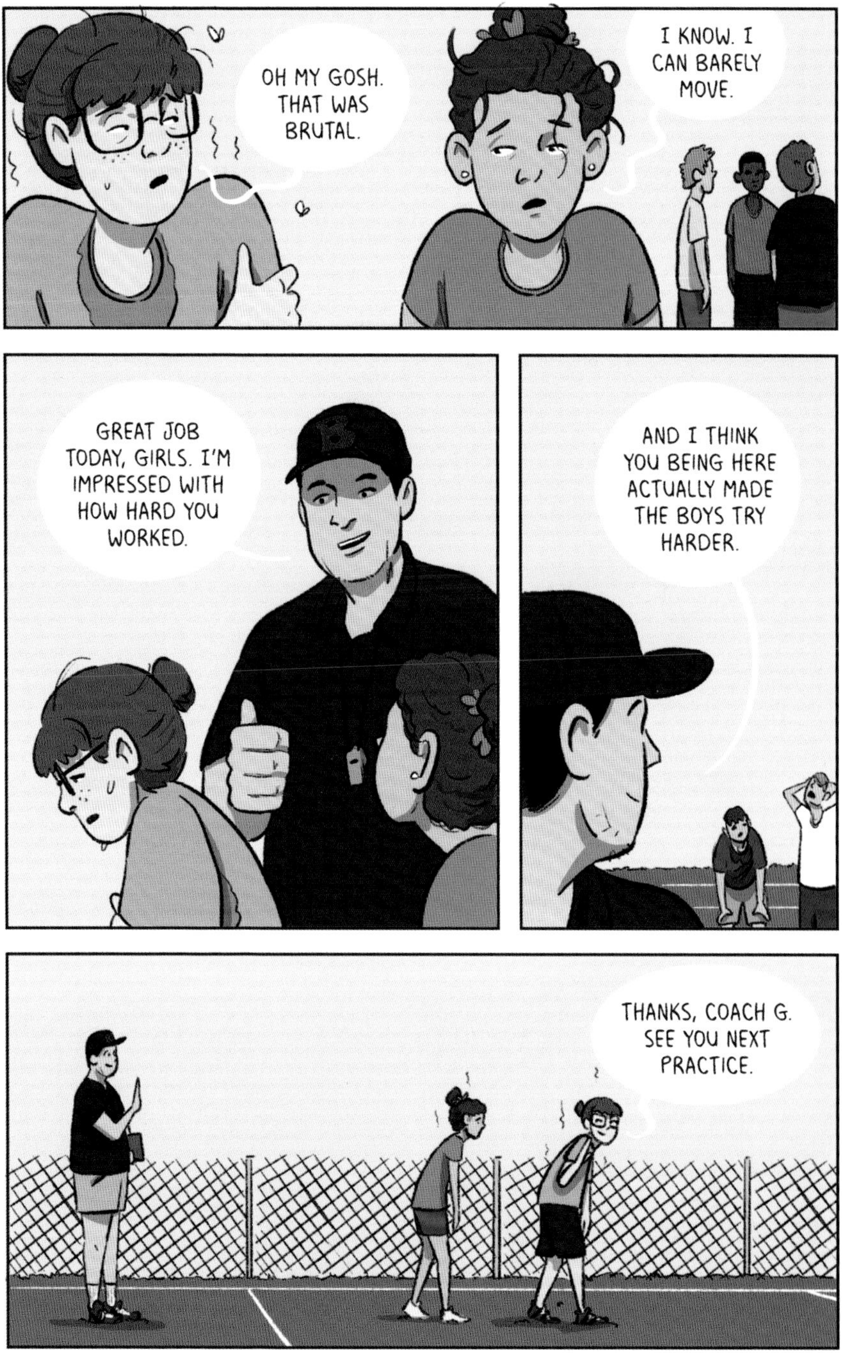
OH MY GOSH. THAT WAS BRUTAL.
I KNOW. I CAN BARELY MOVE.
GREAT JOB TODAY, GIRLS. I'M IMPRESSED WITH HOW HARD YOU WORKED.
AND I THINK YOU BEING HERE ACTUALLY MADE THE BOYS TRY HARDER.
THANKS, COACH G. SEE YOU NEXT PRACTICE.

THAT WAS TERRIFIC! I KNOW IT WAS TOUGH, BUT YOU DID IT!

WOWZERS, WE NEED TO GET YOU TWO HOME. YOU SMELL AWFUL!

IN FACT, I MIGHT HAVE TO SPRAY YOU DOWN WITH THE HOSE OUTSIDE SO YOU DON'T STINK UP THE WHOLE HOUSE...

HA-HA. VERY FUNNY.

CRAIG WAS RIGHT. WE DID SMELL HORRIBLE.

BUT WE DID SOMETHING AWESOME BY FINISHING OUR FIRST PRACTICE—EVEN IF MY LEGS DID FEEL LIKE COOKED SPAGHETTI NOODLES NOW.

AND, YEAH, A BUNCH OF THE BOYS DIDN'T WANT US ON THE TEAM, BUT WE WEREN'T GONNA QUIT.

BREE AND I WOULD JUST HAVE TO WORK HARDER AND GET BETTER.

THEY WEREN'T GONNA GET RID OF US THAT EASILY.

OVER THE NEXT TWO WEEKS, I WORKED MY BUTT OFF TO GET BETTER, STRONGER, FASTER.

TWO MORE, BREE! COME ON! YOU'VE GOT THIS!

WE'LL EAT SO MANY BURRITOS AFTER THIS!

OH, I THINK LUKE'S WATCHING YOU!

NO MATTER HOW I TRIED TO MOTIVATE BREE...

...SHE JUST WOULDN'T GIVE IT HER ALL.

SO I GOT BETTER AT KEEPING UP WITH THE BOYS...

WHICH ONE SHOULD I WEAR TO PRACTICE? WHICH ONE DO YOU THINK THE BOYS WILL THINK IS CUTER?

I DUNNO. DOUBT THEY CARE...

YOU'RE NO HELP.

...AND BREE GOT BETTER AT, WELL, BEING BREE, I GUESS.

39

AS FRUSTRATED AS I WAS ABOUT BREE GIVING UP AT EVERY PRACTICE, I STILL WANTED HER ON THE TEAM. HAVING MY BEST FRIEND THERE MADE FACING THE BOYS A LITTLE EASIER.

AND I WAS AFRAID IF SHE DIDN'T GET BETTER, SHE WAS GONNA QUIT.

HEY!

OH NO... NOT FOOTBALL **AGAIN**...

WHAT?

I THOUGHT WE COULD PRACTICE A LITTLE BEFORE DINNER...

...TOSS THE BALL AROUND...

...MAYBE GO FOR A RUN...

UM... I HAVE A **WAY** BETTER IDEA.

OKAY, IT'S JUST THAT YOU KIND OF SAT ON THE SIDELINES A LOT DURING CONDITIONING, SO I WAS THINKING IF WE WORKED OUT MORE, MAYBE—

WE FINALLY GET A BREAK, MISTY. I DON'T WANT TO WORK OUT.

FINE, BUT, YOU KNOW, CHARLIE MADE IT SOUND LIKE CONDITIONING IS THE WORST PART OF FOOTBALL. YOU MIGHT END UP LIKING IT ONCE WE ACTUALLY START.

SURE, MAYBE...

OKAY. SO, WHAT'S **YOUR** AWESOME IDEA?

THIS IS WHY YOU'RE MY BEST FRIEND.

OH, AND WE CAN'T FORGET THE...

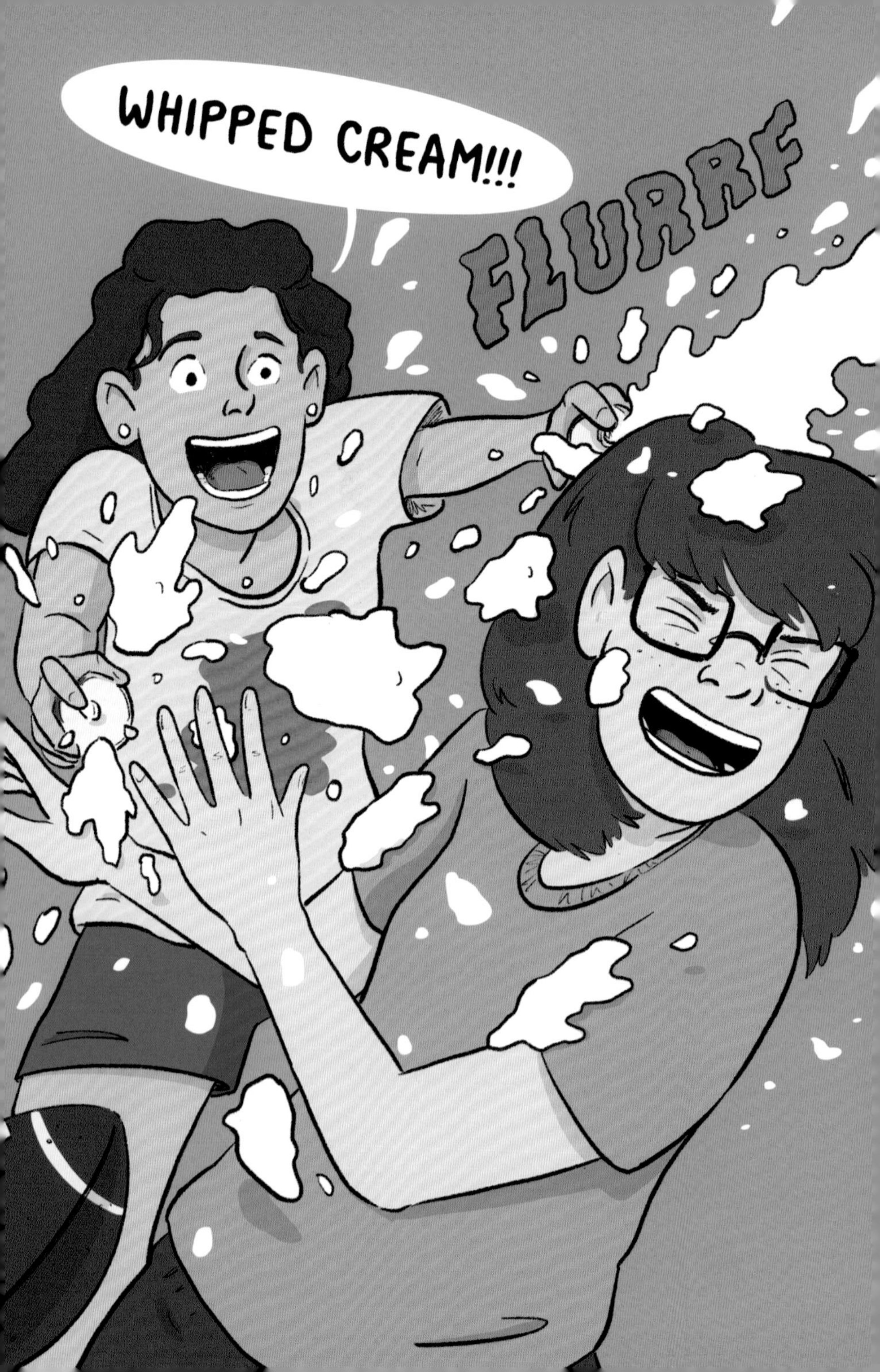
WHIPPED CREAM!!!
FLURRF

ALL RIGHT, I'M GOING TO AVA'S LATER, SO I HAVE TO GO SHOWER REAL QUICK.

YOU'RE GOING TO AVA'S?! CAN I COME?

UM... I THINK IT'D BE A LITTLE WEIRD TO INVITE YOU TO SOMEONE ELSE'S HOUSE, YA KNOW?

OH. RIGHT...

MAYBE NEXT TIME, THOUGH.

YEAH, SURE.

IT BUGGED ME THAT BREE WAS HANGING OUT WITH AVA WITHOUT ME.

I KNEW THEY WERE FRIENDS NOW, BUT HAD SHE EVEN ASKED AVA IF I COULD COME?

IT WAS SORT OF HARD NOT TO WORRY THAT I WAS BEING LEFT OUT ON PURPOSE.

OKAY! ARE YOU READY FOR SOME KARAOKE?

ALWAYS!

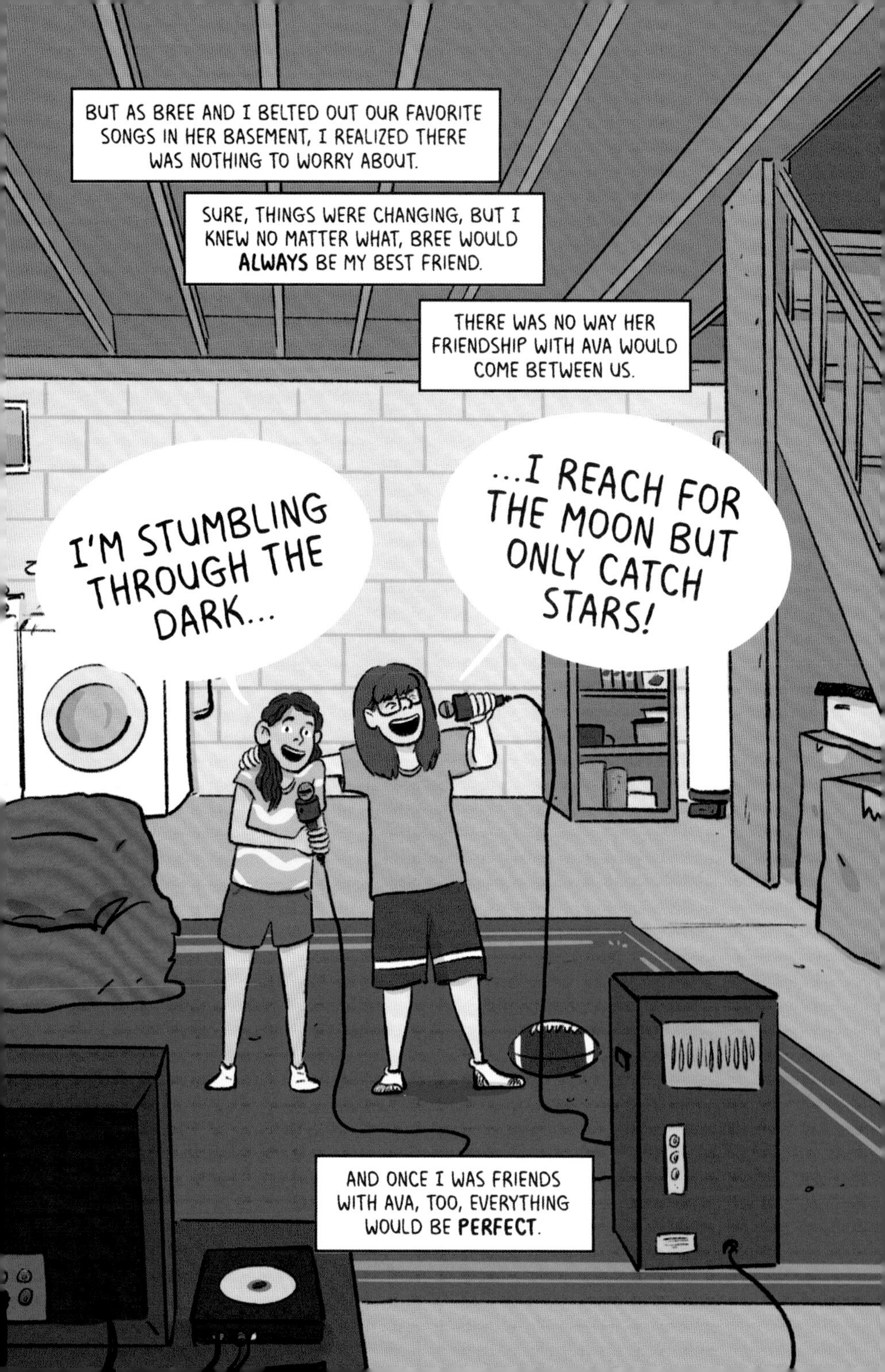
BUT AS BREE AND I BELTED OUT OUR FAVORITE SONGS IN HER BASEMENT, I REALIZED THERE WAS NOTHING TO WORRY ABOUT.
SURE, THINGS WERE CHANGING, BUT I KNEW NO MATTER WHAT, BREE WOULD **ALWAYS** BE MY BEST FRIEND.
THERE WAS NO WAY HER FRIENDSHIP WITH AVA WOULD COME BETWEEN US.
I'M STUMBLING THROUGH THE DARK...
...I REACH FOR THE MOON BUT ONLY CATCH STARS!
AND ONCE I WAS FRIENDS WITH AVA, TOO, EVERYTHING WOULD BE **PERFECT**.

CHAPTER 3

IT WAS FINALLY HERE—THE FIRST DAY OF FULL CONTACT!

BUT BEFORE WE COULD GET STARTED, WE NEEDED GEAR.

THERE ARE SO MANY PADS...

I DON'T GET IT. WHY ARE THERE SHORTS AND PANTS?

UGH, DARN GLASSES.

WHAT IS THIS?

EW! GROSS!

IT WAS HARD TO KNOW WHAT WENT WHERE. WE DIDN'T USE ANY OF THIS STUFF WHEN WE PLAYED AT SCHOOL.

I HOPED THE COACHES WOULD HELP US BEFORE ANY OF THE BOYS SAW US. I DIDN'T WANT THEM TO KNOW HOW CLUELESS WE WERE.

DO YOU GUYS NEED SOME HELP?

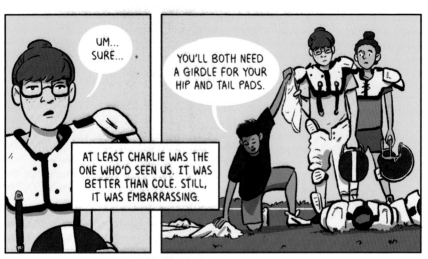

UM... SURE...

YOU'LL BOTH NEED A GIRDLE FOR YOUR HIP AND TAIL PADS.

AT LEAST CHARLIE WAS THE ONE WHO'D SEEN US. IT WAS BETTER THAN COLE. STILL, IT WAS EMBARRASSING.

?

IT GOES UNDER YOUR PANTS.

OH. RIGHT.

I TOTALLY KNEW THAT.

UH-HUH...

AND YOU'LL NEED PANTS THAT ACTUALLY FIT.

THESE THIGH AND KNEE PADS GO INTO THE POCKETS THAT ARE BUILT INTO THE INSIDES OF THE PANTS.

OHHHHH...

MISTY, YOUR SHOULDER PADS ARE ON BACKWARD.

OH.

HEH...

OH, AND DON'T FORGET TO GRAB A JERSEY.

THANKS, CHARLIE.

CHARLIE'S CUTE, DON'T YA THINK?

OH... ER... I DON'T... UH...

OHHH, YOU'RE SO RED! DOES SOMEONE HAVE **A CRUSH?**

WHAT!

NO!

CHILL! I'M JUST KIDDING. I KNOW YOU DON'T **LIKE** BOYS. JEEZ.

THE THING IS, I **DID** LIKE BOYS. I JUST NEVER TOLD BREE WHEN I DID. SHE WAS ALWAYS MAKING MEAN COMMENTS ABOUT MY FRECKLES OR MY HAIR OR MAKING ME FEEL WEIRD ABOUT NOT BEING "GIRLY" ENOUGH.

SHE MADE ME FEEL LIKE I **SHOULDN'T** LIKE ANYONE BECAUSE THEY'D NEVER LIKE ME BACK. SO I ALWAYS KEPT IT A SECRET.

COME TO THINK OF IT, WE HAVE A LOT OF CUTE BOYS ON OUR TEAM.

CAN'T STOP

OKAY, SURE. NOW GET YOUR HEAD IN THE GAME!

SIGH...

IT'S NOT EVEN A GAME...

ONCE EVERYONE WAS READY, IT WAS TIME FOR THE REAL FUN TO BEGIN.

LINE UP, GUYS! AHEM... AND GIRLS.

OR SO I THOUGHT...

LET'S GET WARMED UP!

BUT DOING DRILLS IN PADS WAS SO MUCH HARDER. I COULD BARELY MOVE!

AT LEAST I KNOW THE HELMET WORKS...

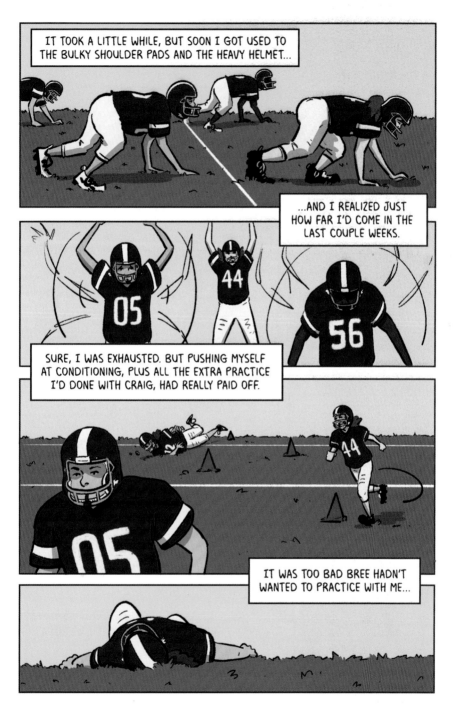

IT TOOK A LITTLE WHILE, BUT SOON I GOT USED TO THE BULKY SHOULDER PADS AND THE HEAVY HELMET...

...AND I REALIZED JUST HOW FAR I'D COME IN THE LAST COUPLE WEEKS.

SURE, I WAS EXHAUSTED. BUT PUSHING MYSELF AT CONDITIONING, PLUS ALL THE EXTRA PRACTICE I'D DONE WITH CRAIG, HAD REALLY PAID OFF.

IT WAS TOO BAD BREE HADN'T WANTED TO PRACTICE WITH ME...

ALL RIGHT! GET SOME WATER!

FINALLY! I THOUGHT THAT WAS NEVER GONNA END!

I KNOW. I'M BEAT!

HA-HA!

HA-HA-HA!

WHAT THE HECK WERE THEY LAUGHING AT? I DIDN'T EVEN DO ANYTHING!

HUH?

NICE HAIR!

OH. YEAH. FUNNY.

BREAK'S OVER!

IT WAS LIKE THEY HAD TO FIND **SOMETHING** TO BE JERKS ABOUT! I'D ALWAYS BEEN SELF-CONSCIOUS ABOUT MY HAIR, BUT THERE WAS NO WAY I WAS GONNA LET THEM KNOW THEY WERE GETTING TO ME.

ALL RIGHT, TEAM! FORM TWO LINES ACROSS FROM EACH OTHER!

TIME FOR TACKLING DRILLS!

YES!

THIS LINE—YOU'RE ON OFFENSE. YOU'LL CARRY THE BALL.

YOU NEED TO GET PAST THE DEFENSIVE PLAYER TO SCORE.

THIS LINE—YOU'RE DEFENSE.

DO NOT LET THE BALL CARRIER GET PAST YOU.

ONCE YOU GO, YOU'LL GET IN THE OTHER LINE.

MISTY AND COLE, YOU'RE UP FIRST.

READY?

I'D BEEN READY SINCE THE FIRST PRACTICE FOR **THIS VERY MOMENT**, BUT I'D BE LYING IF I SAID I WASN'T A LITTLE SCARED...

PREPARE TO BE FLATTENED LIKE A PANCAKE.

HIKE!

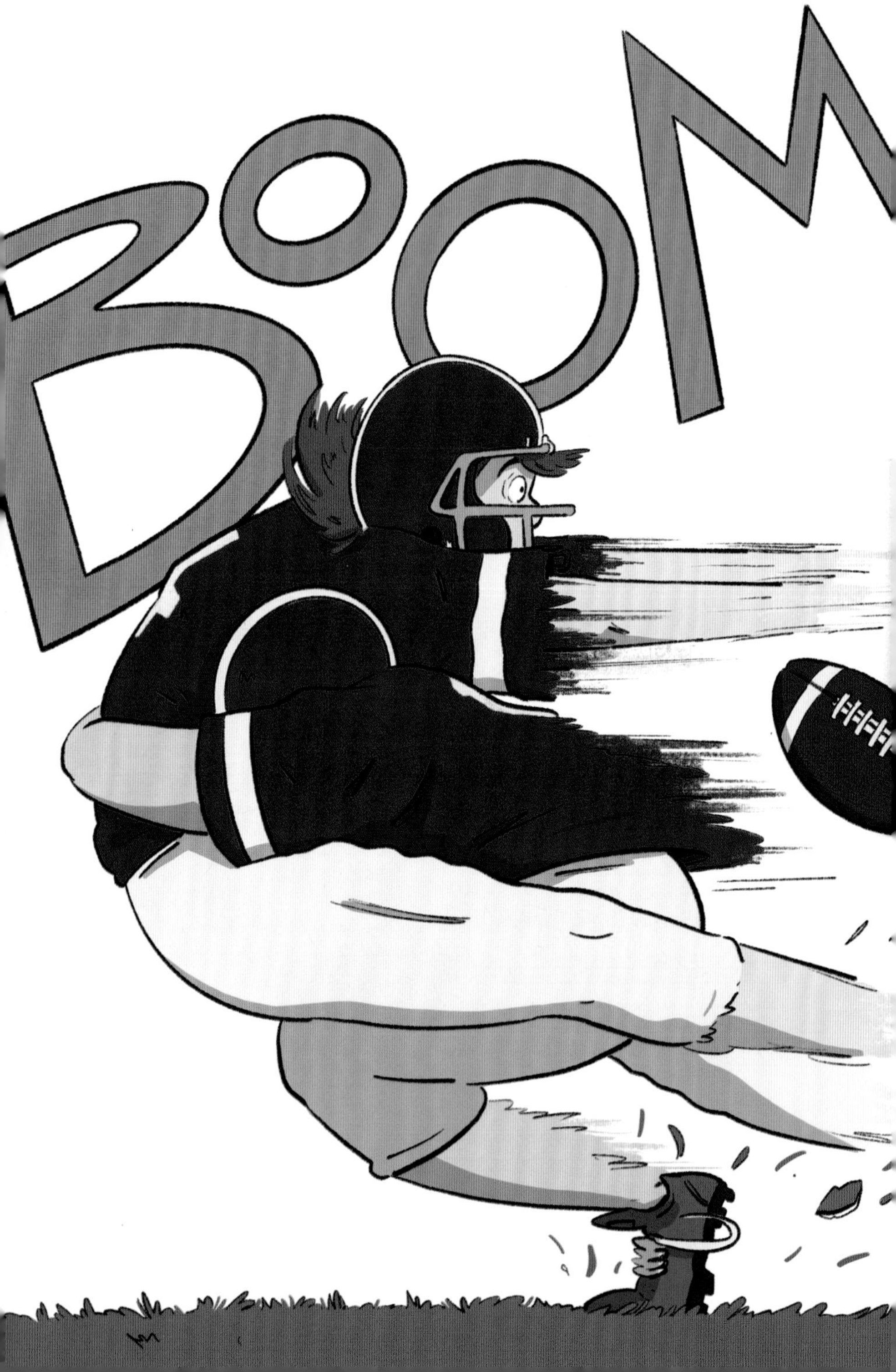
BOOM

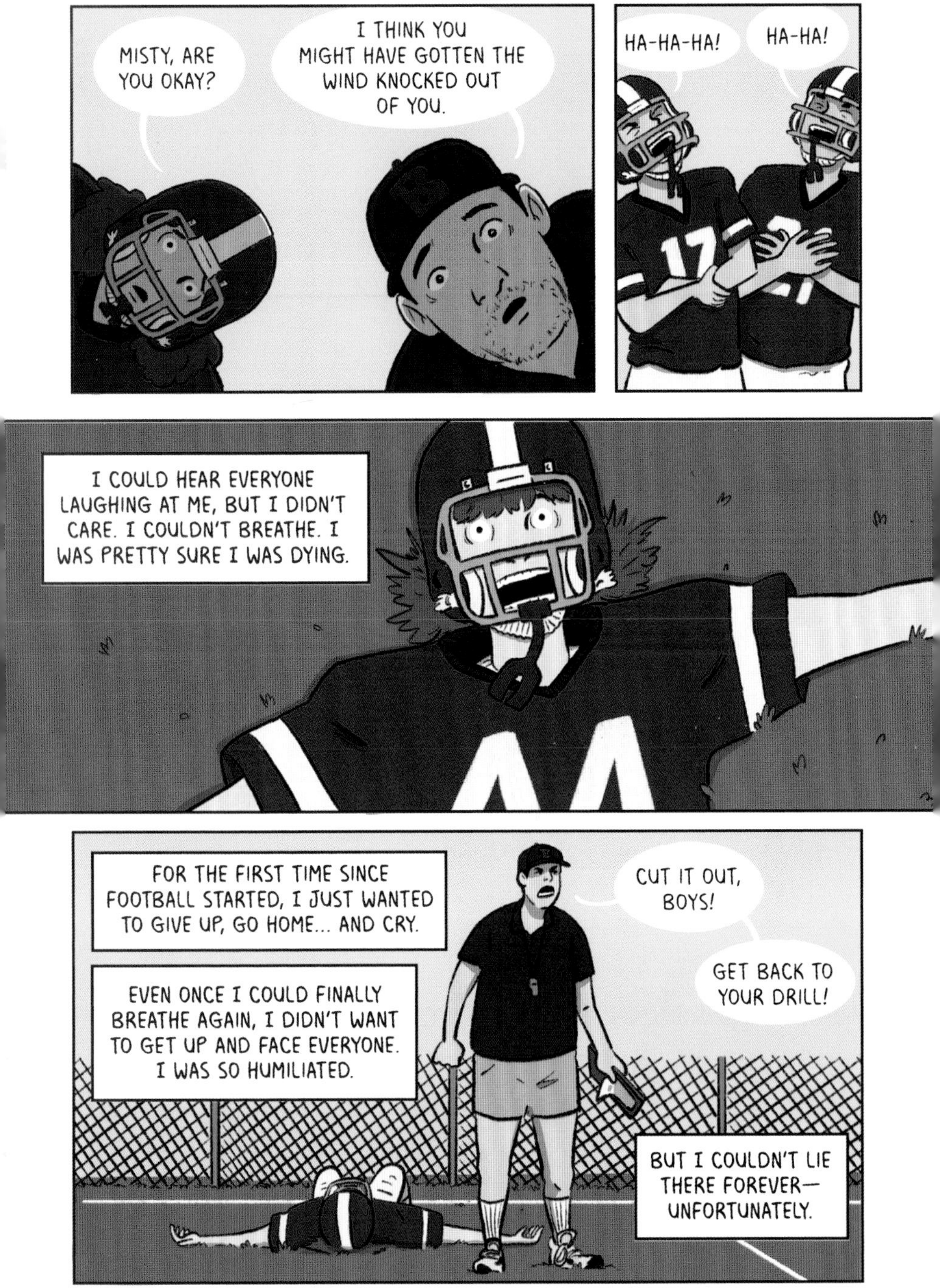
MISTY, ARE YOU OKAY?
I THINK YOU MIGHT HAVE GOTTEN THE WIND KNOCKED OUT OF YOU.
HA-HA-HA!
HA-HA!
I COULD HEAR EVERYONE LAUGHING AT ME, BUT I DIDN'T CARE. I COULDN'T BREATHE. I WAS PRETTY SURE I WAS DYING.
FOR THE FIRST TIME SINCE FOOTBALL STARTED, I JUST WANTED TO GIVE UP, GO HOME... AND CRY.
EVEN ONCE I COULD FINALLY BREATHE AGAIN, I DIDN'T WANT TO GET UP AND FACE EVERYONE. I WAS SO HUMILIATED.
CUT IT OUT, BOYS!
GET BACK TO YOUR DRILL!
BUT I COULDN'T LIE THERE FOREVER—UNFORTUNATELY.

I DON'T THINK I CAN DO THIS...

HUFF

HUFF

HUFF

COUGH I THINK I HAVE A BUG IN MY THROAT. *COUGH* I NEED TO SIT OUT. *COUGH*

ALL RIGHT. JOIN US WHEN YOU'RE READY, I SUPPOSE.

A BUG?! REALLY?! SHE COULDN'T BE SERIOUS!

OKAY, MISTY. MAYBE I SHOULD GIVE YOU A FEW QUICK POINTERS SINCE YOU'RE NEW TO ALL OF THIS.

WHEN YOU'RE TAKING A TACKLE, YOU WANT TO BEND OVER A LITTLE. TRY TO STAY LOW BECAUSE OTHERWISE YOU'LL END UP WITH A HELMET STRAIGHT TO THE GUT.

WHEN YOU'RE RUNNING THE BALL AGAINST A DEFENDER, HOLD IT LIKE THIS. TUCK IT CLOSE TO YOUR BODY AND KEEP A TIGHT GRIP SO YOU DON'T FUMBLE IT.

I KNOW IT'S TOUGH, BUT YOU CAN DO THIS.

COACH G, I'M REALLY NOT SURE I CAN...

BALONEY. LISTEN, IN A FEW MINUTES, YOU'RE GOING TO FEEL BETTER.

THEN I WANT YOU TO GO OUT THERE AND HAND IT BACK TO THOSE BOYS.

BECAUSE FOOTBALL IS ALL ABOUT GETTING KNOCKED DOWN AND GETTING BACK UP AGAIN.

AND YOU DON'T STRIKE ME AS THE TYPE OF PERSON WHO STAYS DOWN OR QUITS WHEN THINGS GET HARD.

SO IT'S TIME TO GO OUT THERE AND SHOW 'EM WHAT YOU'RE MADE OF.

COACH G WAS RIGHT—I WASN'T A QUITTER. BESIDES, ME QUITTING MEANT THEM WINNING, AND I COULDN'T LET THAT HAPPEN.

I HAD TO GET BACK OUT ON THE FIELD AND SHOW THEM JUST HOW **FIERCE** I WAS—EVEN IF I DID FEEL LIKE I'D BEEN RUN OVER BY AN ICE-CREAM TRUCK.

OF COURSE, THE NEXT PERSON I HAD TO FACE WAS COLE'S BEST FRIEND, NICK. HE WAS JUST AS MEAN AS COLE, BUT HE WASN'T AS BIG...

...SO MAYBE THERE WAS HOPE.

HIKE!

BACK FOR MORE, HUH?

...OR NOT.

CRACK!

POP!

READY TO QUIT YET?

29

UGH.

I WAS SO FRUSTRATED, AND EVEN THOUGH SHE HAD NOTHING TO DO WITH IT, BREE SITTING ON THE SIDELINES NOT EVEN TRYING—AGAIN—WAS MAKING ME EVEN CRANKIER.

44

NOW I HAD TO SWITCH LINES, WHICH MEANT IT WAS MY TURN TO DO THE TACKLING...

...BUT IT WAS HARD TO BE EXCITED ABOUT IT WHEN CHANCES WERE, I WAS GONNA BE PULVERIZED, ANYWAY.

HEY, MISTY...

WHAT?!

I WAS JUST GOING TO ASK IF YOU WANTED SOME HELP...

OH...

WAIT.

YOU'RE GONNA HELP ME?

BEN WAS ONE OF CHARLIE'S BEST FRIENDS. ACTUALLY, HE ALSO USED TO BE ONE OF MY FRIENDS, BUT SO FAR, HE HADN'T REALLY TALKED TO ME AT FOOTBALL PRACTICES.

I FIGURED HE HATED ME FOR BEING HERE, TOO.

YEAH, I MEAN, YOU'RE KIND OF A MESS OUT THERE...

YEAH, I KNOW.

BUT MAYBE YOU'LL BE BETTER ON DEFENSE!

LOOK, WHEN YOU'RE TACKLING SOMEONE, YOU WANT TO WRAP YOUR ARMS AROUND BOTH OF THEIR LEGS BECAUSE THEN THEY CAN'T RUN. SIMPLE AS THAT!

OKAY, YEAH, I GUESS THAT SOUNDS SIMPLE.

OKAY, MISTY, YOU'RE UP!

THANKS, BEN!

GOOD LUCK...

I WAS PROBABLY GONNA NEED ALL THE LUCK I COULD GET...

...BECAUSE WHEN IT CAME TO FOOTBALL, LOTS OF THINGS THAT I'D THOUGHT SEEMED SIMPLE HAD TURNED OUT TO BE REALLY HARD.

GO!

BUT THERE WAS SOMETHING ABOUT BEING ON DEFENSE.

THE ADRENALINE RUSH...

...THE CHALLENGE OF STOPPING SOMEONE...

...THE TACKLING!

WOMP

WHOA...

I LOVED IT.

AND I WAS GOOD AT IT.

PRETTY IMPRESSIVE.

THAT WAS AWESOME!

OH, UM, HEH, THANKS, CHARLIE.

MAX LOOKS PRETTY PEEVED YOU JUST TACKLED HIM.

HA! YEAH, HE DOES! I'M GLAD I GOT TO GO AGAINST HIM AND NOT COLE.

YEAH...

COLE'S THE BEST TACKLER ON THE TEAM. IF YOU WANT TO GET PAST HIM, YOU'RE GOING TO HAVE TO JUKE HIM.

JUKE HIM?

YEAH, GET HIM TO THINK YOU'RE GOING ONE WAY, THEN BURST THE OTHER WAY.

YOU KNOW, FAKE HIM OUT.

OH. YEAH, I CAN DO THAT FOR SURE.

A LITTLE WHILE LATER.

MISTY! YOU'RE UP!

COLE, YOU TOO!

STAY LOW.

TUCK THE BALL. FAKE HIM OUT.

LET'S DO THIS.

OKAY, I'LL ADMIT IT. I WAS TERRIFIED. MY STOMACH STILL HURT FROM THE LAST TIME I WAS PITTED AGAINST HIM.

BUT I WAS DETERMINED TO WIPE THAT ANNOYING LOOK OFF HIS FACE.

HIKE!

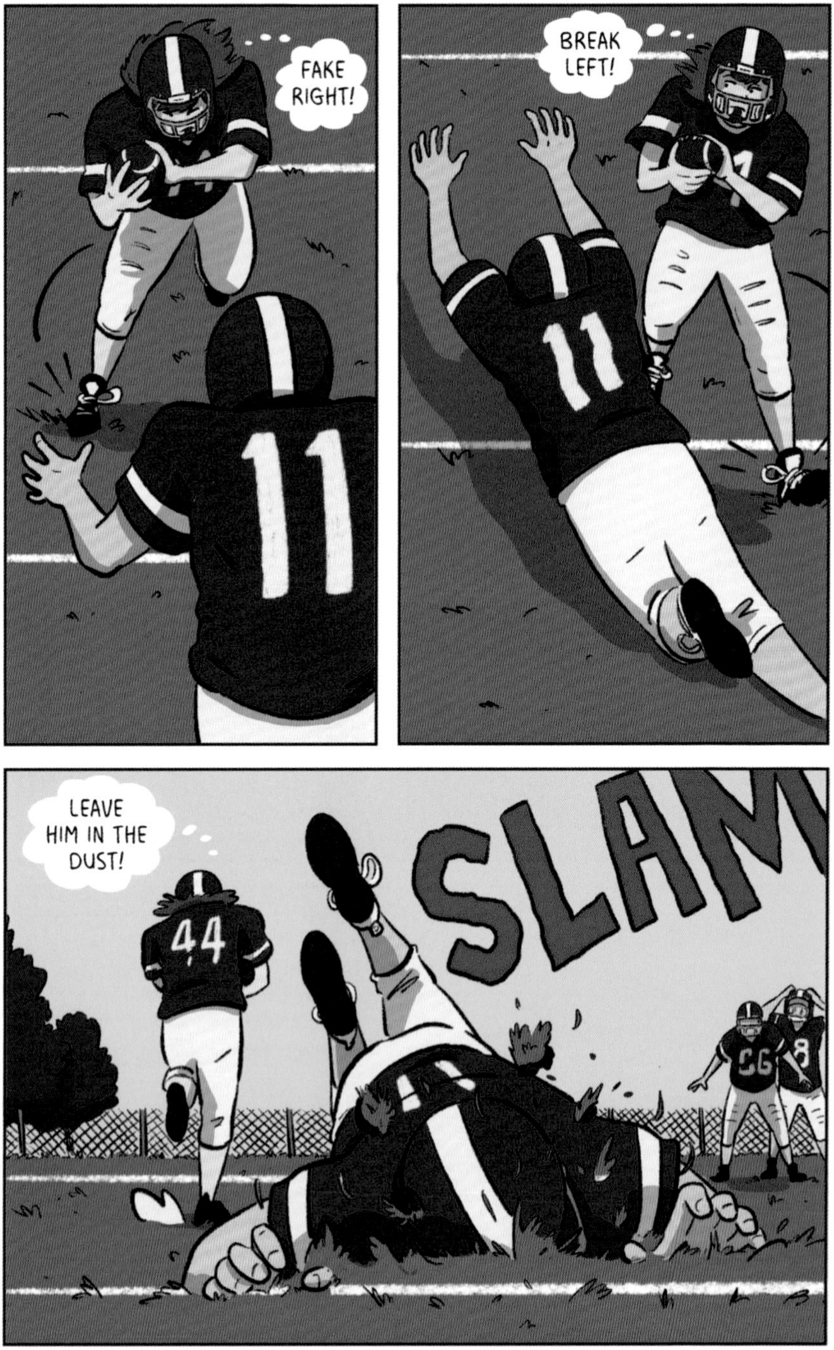
FAKE RIGHT!
BREAK LEFT!
LEAVE HIM IN THE DUST!
SLAM

OHHHHH!!! HE GOT JUKED!

THAT WAS GNARLY!

NO WAY!

I CAN'T BELIEVE IT! SHE DID IT!

I... I DID IT!

PUNCH

PUNCH

PUNCH

COLE WOULD PROBABLY HATE ME MORE NOW, BUT I DIDN'T EVEN CARE. THIS WAS TURNING OUT TO BE THE BEST DAY EVER.

THAT WAS AWESOME!

THANKS, CHARLIE!

AND THERE WAS NO WAY I WAS TELLING BREE, BUT...

...I DEFINITELY LIKED CHARLIE.

AFTER PRACTICE, THINGS BETWEEN BREE AND ME WERE KIND OF WEIRD. I WASN'T REALLY **MAD** AT HER, BUT IT WAS HARD NOT TO BE A LITTLE ANNOYED.

BYE... AND GOOD JOB TODAY.

I WANTED TO TELL HER GOOD JOB, TOO, BUT, WELL, THAT BUG STAYED LODGED IN HER THROAT FOR THE **ENTIRE PRACTICE**, SO...

THANKS... SEE YA TOMORROW...

HI, MISTY! I THOUGHT IT WAS YOU WE SAW ON THE FIELD.

HEH. YEP, IT WAS ME.

JENNA, AMANDA, AND I STARTED GOING TO SCHOOL TOGETHER LAST YEAR AFTER ALL THE ELEMENTARY SCHOOLS MERGED FOR MIDDLE SCHOOL.

I HARDLY KNEW THEM, BUT JENNA WAS ALWAYS TALKING SOMEONE'S EAR OFF IN CLASS, WHILE AMANDA SEEMED MORE SHY.

I'D NOTICED THEM AT CHEER PRACTICE ON THE FIELD NEXT TO OURS, BUT TODAY, I'D REALLY HOPED THEY WOULDN'T NOTICE ME...

...BECAUSE MY HAIR WAS SERIOUSLY EMBARRASSING.

I CAN'T BELIEVE YOU AND BREE ARE PLAYING FOOTBALL.

THAT'S SO COOL!

I KNEW PEOPLE WOULD THINK IT WAS COOL!

THANKS!

SOOOO... WHAT'S IT LIKE PLAYING WITH BEN?

OH MY GOSH, YOU **WOULD** ASK THAT!

WHAT?

BEN'S BEEN HELPFUL, ACTUALLY. BUT ALMOST ALL OF THE OTHER BOYS **REALLY** DON'T WANT ME ON THE TEAM.

YEAH, THEY LOOKED LIKE THEY WERE OUT FOR VENGEANCE TODAY!

WE SAW YOU GET TACKLED AND... **YIKES**!

YEAH, THAT WAS... ROUGH.

UGH, OF COURSE THEY SAW ME GET LAID OUT. THAT WAS MORE EMBARRASSING THAN MY HAIR!

THAT'S ONE GOOD THING ABOUT CHEER—NO TACKLING! I COULD NEVER!

ME NEITHER!

I DON'T KNOW. I'VE SEEN YOU DO SOME PRETTY WILD LIFTS AND FLIPS, AND THAT STUFF SEEMS HARD, TOO.

I DIDN'T REALIZE CHEERLEADERS DID ALL THAT.

YEAH, SOME OF US HAVE A CHEER COMPETITION COMING UP, SO WE'RE TRYING TO PERFECT OUR STUNTS.

WHAT?! CHEERLEADERS **COMPETE**? I DIDN'T KNOW THAT.

YEAH, IT CAN GET REALLY INTENSE.

I THINK WE MIGHT HAVE A CHANCE AT FIRST PLACE!

DARN IT, I GOTTA GO.

HONK HONK

OKAY. SEE YOU NEXT PRACTICE!

I COULDN'T WAIT TO TELL BREE THAT GIRLS FROM SCHOOL THOUGHT IT WAS COOL THAT WE WERE PLAYING FOOTBALL!

MAYBE IT WOULD CONVINCE HER TO TRY HARDER AT PRACTICE...

BUT THAT NIGHT AT BREE'S, I DIDN'T GET A CHANCE TO TELL HER ABOUT JENNA AND AMANDA BECAUSE **NOTHING** WENT AS PLANNED...

I'M QUITTING FOOTBALL.

NO! COME ON!

I KNOW IT'S TOUGH, BUT I TOLD YOU I'LL PRACTICE WITH YOU. IT'LL GET EASIER.

THAT'S NOT WHY I'M QUITTING.

THEN WHY?

I THOUGHT WE WERE GONNA DO THIS TOGETHER.

SIGH...

I FEEL LIKE WE NEVER HAVE TIME TO JUST HANG OUT ANYMORE. I'D RATHER BE DOING THINGS WITH FRIENDS THAN BE AT FOOTBALL. THAT'S ALL.

I'M YOUR FRIEND. YOUR BEST FRIEND. WE HANG OUT **AT** FOOTBALL.

SEE?

YOU CAN DO BOTH.

I MEAN **OTHER** FRIENDS.

THAT'S WHEN I REALIZED I DIDN'T REALLY HAVE OTHER FRIENDS.

BESIDES, AVA SAYS NO BOYS WILL LIKE US AS LONG AS WE'RE PLAYING FOOTBALL.

WAIT. WHY WOULD SHE SAY "US"?! DOES SHE STILL THINK I LIKE CHARLIE?!

AND IS THAT TRUE?

WILL CHARLIE REALLY NEVER LIKE ME IF I'M ON THE TEAM?

I KNOW YOU DON'T CARE ABOUT THAT, BUT I DO.

I DON'T UNDERSTAND WHY YOU WANT TO KEEP PLAYING WHEN THEY'RE ALL SO MEAN TO US.

NOT **ALL** THE BOYS ARE MEAN. CHARLIE AND BEN HAVE BEEN NICE...

AND I LIKE FOOTBALL! I WANT TO BE GOOD AT IT.

PLEASE DON'T QUIT. WITH MORE PRACTICE, WE CAN **BOTH** BE GOOD—MAYBE EVEN THE BEST ON THE TEAM.

UGH.

YOU MAKE EVERYTHING INTO A COMPETITION! YOU DO IT AT RECESS, AND YOU EVEN DO IT IN SCHOOL!

YOU DON'T ALWAYS HAVE TO BE THE BEST AT EVERYTHING, MISTY!

I'LL NEVER BE GOOD AT IT. I DON'T WANT TO BE. I DON'T CARE ABOUT FOOTBALL.

DON'T YOU GET THAT?

I GUESS...

BUT I WAS THINKING, WHAT IF YOU QUIT WITH ME?

WE'D HAVE MORE TIME TO DO ACTUAL FUN STUFF. YOU KNOW, LIKE WE USED TO. AND WE COULD HANG OUT WITH AVA.

OBVIOUSLY, I WANTED TO BE FRIENDS WITH AVA, BUT THAT DIDN'T MEAN I HAD TO CHOOSE. I KNEW I COULD PLAY FOOTBALL **AND** MAKE TIME TO HANG OUT.

I DON'T WANT TO QUIT, BUT WHY DON'T WE DO SOMETHING TOMORROW? YOU, ME, AND AVA.

WELL, WE WERE GOING TO GO TO THE MALL FOR NEW SCHOOL CLOTHES...

...BUT YOU HATE SHOPPING...

NO, THE MALL SOUNDS GREAT. WE'LL HAVE A BLAST!

BOING

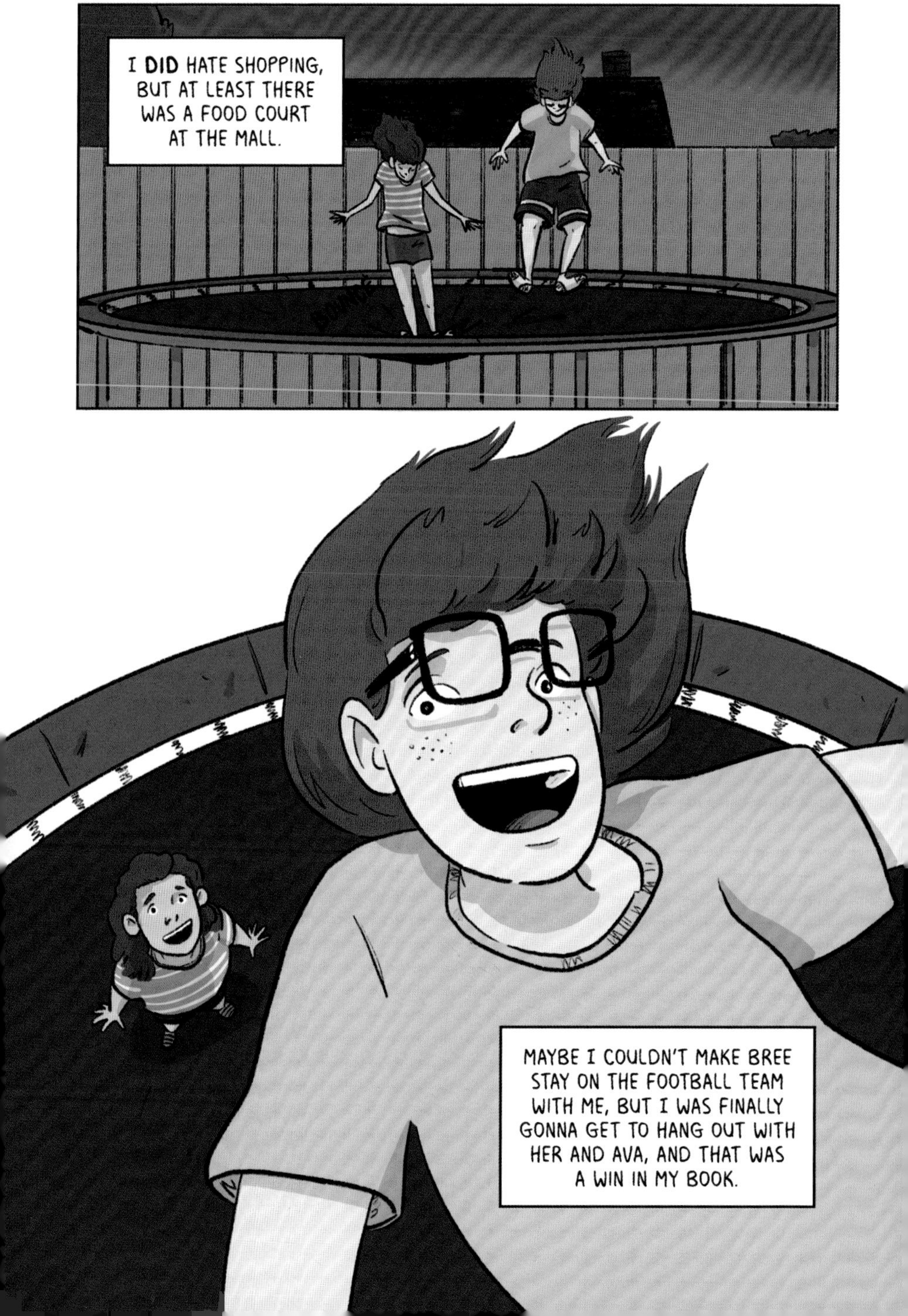
I **DID** HATE SHOPPING, BUT AT LEAST THERE WAS A FOOD COURT AT THE MALL.
MAYBE I COULDN'T MAKE BREE STAY ON THE FOOTBALL TEAM WITH ME, BUT I WAS FINALLY GONNA GET TO HANG OUT WITH HER AND AVA, AND THAT WAS A WIN IN MY BOOK.

THE NEXT DAY, AVA'S MOM TOOK US TO THE MALL.

LET'S START IN THE JUNIORS DEPARTMENT!

OKAY, AND I WANT TO CHECK OUT THE SHOES.

ISN'T THIS SOOOO CUTE?!

I LOVE IT!

HAVING TO WALK AROUND STORES FOR HOURS, PRETENDING TO LIKE THE CLOTHES THEY PICKED OUT, WAS BASICALLY MY WORST NIGHTMARE.

BUT I WANTED TO FIT IN, SO...

SO CUTE!

YOU REALLY THINK SO, MISTY?

FOR SURE!

I THOUGHT YOU ONLY LIKED, YOU KNOW, BASKETBALL SHORTS.

OH, NO. I LIKE ALL SORTS OF CLOTHES!

MAYBE YOU SHOULD PICK OUT SOMETHING ELSE TO WEAR, THEN.

YOU'VE BEEN WEARING THE SAME CLOTHES FOR LIKE THE LAST THREE YEARS.

OH...

YEAH, MAYBE I SHOULD...

BREE WAS BEING **SO MEAN** AROUND AVA, BUT EVEN THOUGH SHE'D HURT MY FEELINGS, I DIDN'T WANT TO SEEM OVERLY SENSITIVE, SO I DIDN'T SAY ANYTHING.

(BUT, FOR THE RECORD, WHAT SHE'D SAID WASN'T EVEN TRUE. I WON THIS SHIRT LAST SUMMER AT BASKETBALL CAMP!)

WHAT DO YOU THINK OF THIS?

YEAH, GROSS, RIGHT?

I CAN'T BELIEVE THEY EVEN SELL THIS UGLY THING.

I KIND OF LIKED THE SHIRT...

THIS IS CUTE!

BUT APPARENTLY I LIKED CLOTHES THAT OTHER GIRLS THOUGHT WERE UGLY...

...SO I GUESS IT WAS A GOOD THING I WAS SHOPPING WITH AVA. IF I WANTED TO LOOK CUTE, ALL I HAD TO DO WAS COPY HER.

SO, MISTY, ARE YOU GOING TO START WEARING CONTACTS NOW THAT YOU'RE GETTING USED TO THEM AT FOOTBALL?

I DON'T KNOW.

I'M NOT SURE I'LL EVER GET USED TO FINGERS TOUCHING MY EYEBALLS.

I JUST DON'T HAVE A CHOICE AT FOOTBALL.

IF YOU ASK ME, YOU'RE BETTER OFF WEARING YOUR GLASSES. YOUR UNIBROW ISN'T AS NOTICEABLE.

SERIOUSLY?! WHY WOULD AVA EVEN WANT TO BE FRIENDS WITH SOMEONE THIS MEAN?

UGH. SPEAKING OF EYEBROWS, I SHOULD PROBABLY PLUCK MINE, TOO.

WHATEVER.

YOUR EYEBROWS ARE PERFECT.

I GUESS THAT EXPLAINED IT.

AW, THANKS!

HEY, LET'S LOOK AT MAKEUP! I NEED SOME NEW LIP GLOSS.

GREAT. I DIDN'T KNOW THE FIRST THING ABOUT MAKEUP—OR EVEN HOW TO BE A GIRL, APPARENTLY.

THERE WAS SO MUCH STUFF I WAS SUPPOSED TO THINK ABOUT NOW—LIKE MY **EYEBROWS.**

I MEAN, THEY WERE A LITTLE BUSHY...

...AND I **HAD** GOTTEN LOTS OF ZITS FROM SWEATING UNDER MY FOOTBALL HELMET. MAKEUP **WOULD** HELP COVER THEM UP...

ACTUALLY, A COMPLETE MAKEOVER WOULD PROBABLY HELP ME FIT IN BETTER WITH AVA. I WAS ALREADY GETTING NEW CLOTHES. I COULD JUST TAKE IT A STEP FURTHER...

MAYBE I COULD EVEN GO BLOND!

SALE

PONTENE V6

MY NEW MALL MISSION: GATHER WHAT I NEEDED FOR A WHOLE NEW ME.

AFTER OUR SHOPPING SPREE, IT SEEMED LIKE BREE WAS ALWAYS TOO "BUSY" FOR ME. SHE HADN'T INVITED ME OVER IN ALMOST A WHOLE WEEK!

WHY ARE YOU MOPING AROUND THE HOUSE TODAY?

BREE SAID SHE COULDN'T COME OVER TODAY. SHE'S AT THE MOVIES WITH AVA... AGAIN.

AND I WASN'T INVITED... AGAIN.

OH, I'M SORRY. MAYBE TALK TO HER ABOUT IT IF IT'S BOTHERING YOU.

IN THE MEANTIME, I'M SURE YOUR SISTER WOULD LOVE TO PLAY WITH YOU.

YEAH! WANNA PLAY BARBIES?! YOU CAN BE MERMAID BARBIE—SHE'S THE BEST!

I DON'T PLAY WITH BARBIES ANYMORE.

OH, I KNOW, MOM!

DO YOU WANNA WATCH A MOVIE WHILE THE TWINS ARE NAPPING?

WE HAVEN'T DONE THAT IN A WHILE.

I'M REALLY SORRY, HONEY, BUT I'M EXHAUSTED. I REALLY WANT TO TAKE A NAP WHILE THEY'RE SLEEPING. IT'S THE ONLY CHANCE I GET SOMETIMES.

FINE.

WHY DON'T YOU INVITE OVER THOSE CHEERLEADER GIRLS YOU TOLD ME ABOUT?

OR MAYBE CRAIG WILL PLAY FOOTBALL WITH YOU IN THE BACKYARD.

YES! LET'S GO!

CRAIG AND I HAD BEEN SPENDING A LOT OF TIME TOGETHER SINCE I STARTED PLAYING FOOTBALL.

IT WAS AWESOME HAVING SOMEONE WHO WANTED TO HELP ME PRACTICE...

NICE THROW!

...BUT I SORT OF WISHED BREE WEREN'T MY **ONLY** FRIEND, SO I HAD SOMEONE ELSE TO HANG OUT WITH WHEN SHE WAS WITH AVA.

I GUESS I WAS GONNA HAVE TO TACKLE MAKING FRIENDS THE SAME WAY I TACKLED PLAYING FOOTBALL—BY JUST GOING FOR IT!

WOMP

CHAPTER 4

A FEW DAYS LATER, I HAD MY LAST PRACTICE BEFORE SCHOOL STARTED.

I WAS PANICKING WITHOUT BREE. WHO WOULD BE MY STRETCHING PARTNER? WHO WOULD I COMPLAIN WITH?

HEY, MISTY.

IS BREE SICK OR SOMETHIN'?

YEAH, SICK OF FOOTBALL!

...

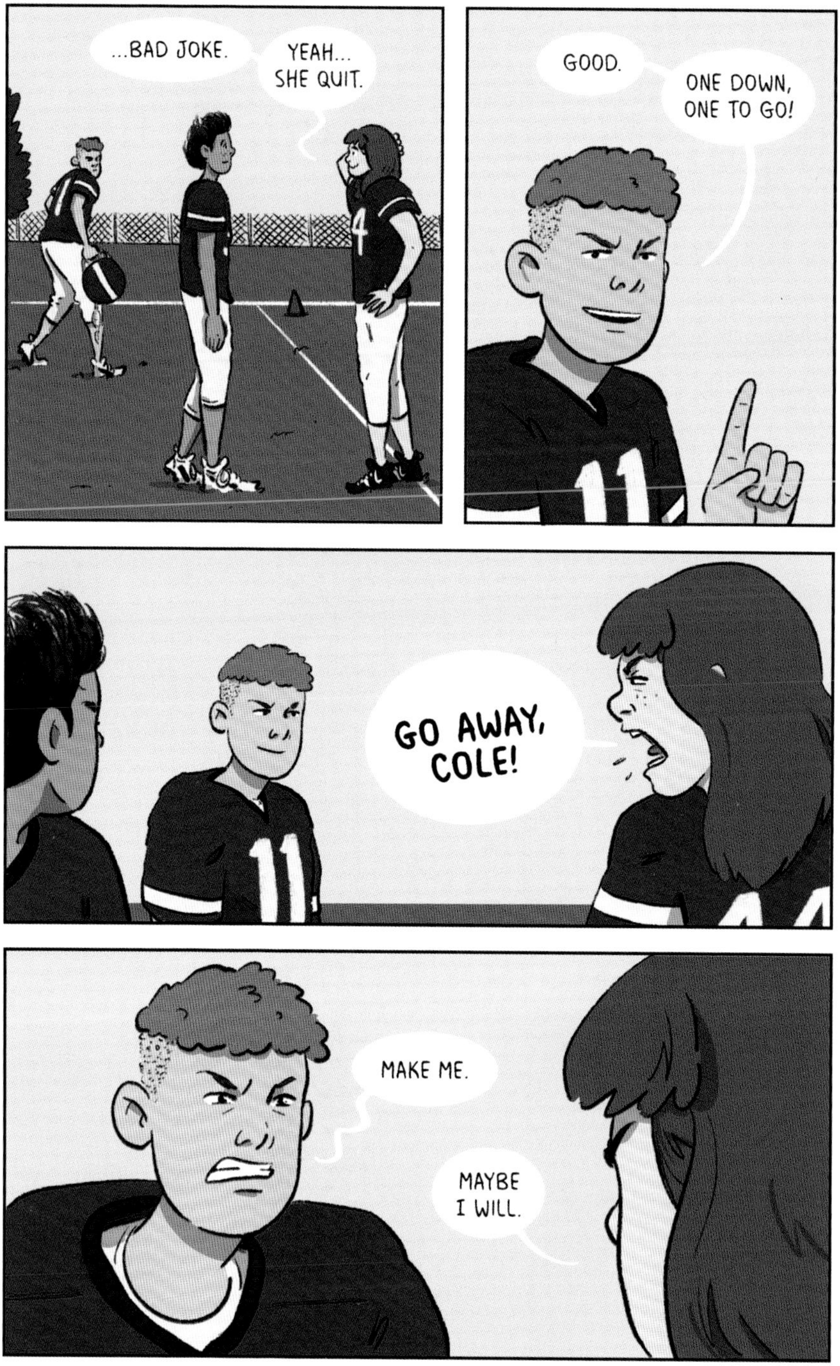
...BAD JOKE.
YEAH... SHE QUIT.
GOOD.
ONE DOWN, ONE TO GO!
GO AWAY, COLE!
MAKE ME.
MAYBE I WILL.

OKAY, TEAM. LET'S GET WARMED UP!

WHAT A JERK.

I'LL BE YOUR PARTNER FOR STRETCHING TODAY IF YOU WANT.

OH...

PLAY IT COOL, MISTY...

UH...

YES!

UM...

OKAY...

LATER.

CIRCLE UP, TEAM! I'M GOING TO ANNOUNCE YOUR POSITIONS FOR THE SEASON.

I DIDN'T KNOW **EXACTLY** WHICH POSITION I WANTED, BUT I KNEW I LOVED TACKLING, WHICH MEANT ONE THING...

DEFENSE. DEFENSE. DEFENSE.

MISTY, YOU'RE ON OFFENSE.

RIGHT TACKLE.

OFFENSE?!

THE WEIRD THING ABOUT MY NEW POSITION WAS THAT EVEN THOUGH IT'S CALLED A TACKLE, YOU DON'T ACTUALLY GET TO TACKLE.

THE OFFENSIVE TACKLE IS ONE OF THE LINEMEN. THEY HAVE AN IMPORTANT JOB: TO BLOCK THE PLAYERS ON THE OTHER TEAM FROM GETTING TO THE PLAYER WITH THE BALL—USUALLY THE QUARTERBACK OR THE RUNNING BACK.

THE OFFENSIVE LINE STANDS OPPOSITE THE OTHER TEAM'S DEFENSIVE LINE. THE RIGHT TACKLE SPECIFICALLY FACES THE OTHER TEAM'S BEST RUN STOPPERS.

IN ADDITION TO PROTECTING THE QUARTERBACK, THE OFFENSIVE TACKLE HAS TO BE ABLE TO CREATE A PATH, OR HOLE, FOR THE RUNNING BACK TO RUN THROUGH.

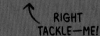

OFFENSIVE LINE

RIGHT TACKLE—ME!

QUARTERBACK—THROWS, HANDS OFF, OR RUNS THE BALL. ALSO CALLS THE PLAYS.

RUNNING BACK—RUNS THE BALL TO THE END ZONE.

SO, SURE, IT WASN'T DEFENSE, BUT IT WAS STILL PRETTY AWESOME.

ALL RIGHT, TEAM. LET'S RUN SOME PLAYS! AFTER THIS GROUP GOES, THE BOYS ON THE SIDELINES WILL ROTATE IN.

GOT IT? LET'S GO!

I WAS TOTALLY FREAKING OUT...

...BECAUSE, OF COURSE, THE DEFENDER IN FRONT OF ME HAPPENED TO BE COLE.

HIKE!

JUST...

QUIT...

ALREADY!

THUMP

95

UGH! WHY'D HE HAVE TO MAKE EVERYTHING SO HARD **ALL THE TIME?**

LET'S GO AGAIN.

HIKE!

RAM

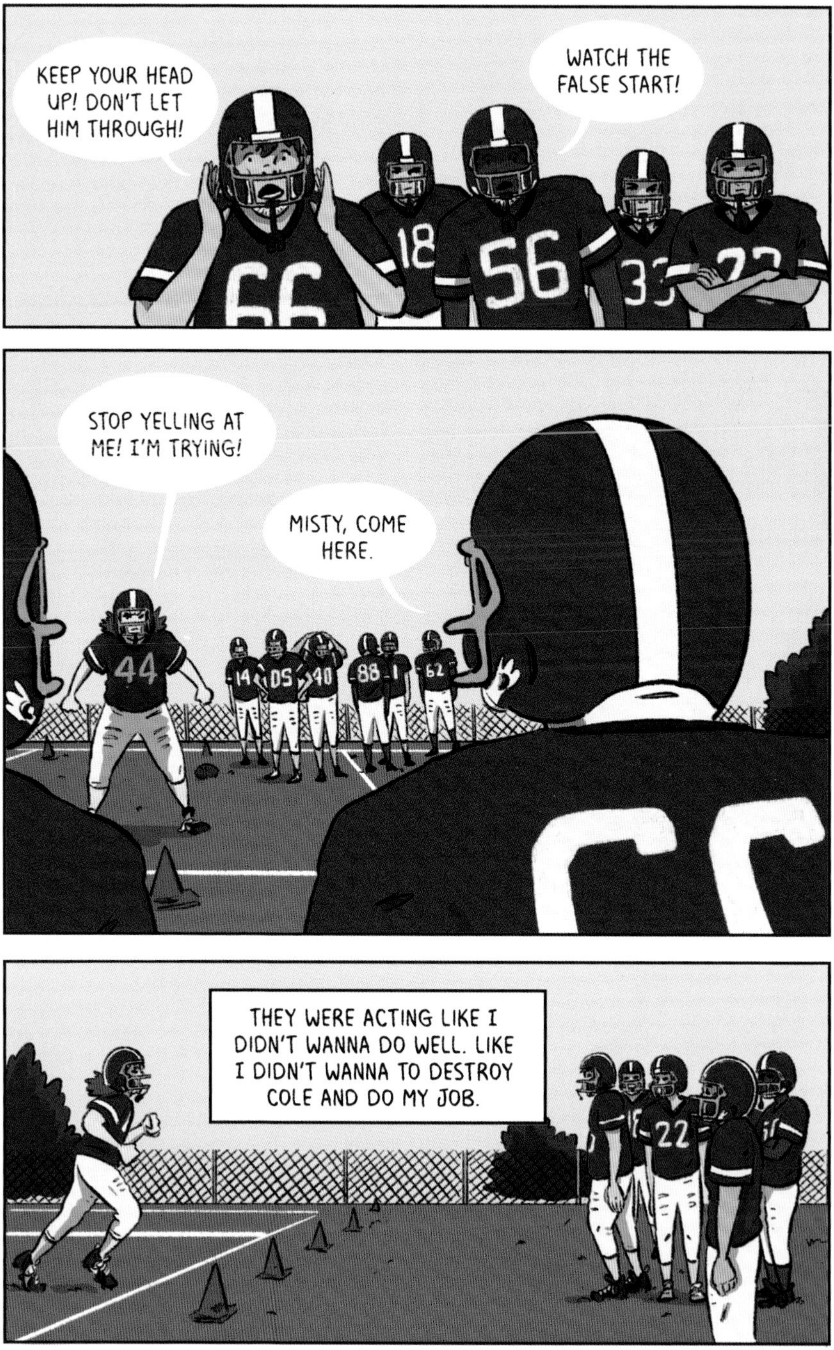
KEEP YOUR HEAD UP! DON'T LET HIM THROUGH!
WATCH THE FALSE START!
STOP YELLING AT ME! I'M TRYING!
MISTY, COME HERE.
THEY WERE ACTING LIKE I DIDN'T WANNA DO WELL. LIKE I DIDN'T WANNA TO DESTROY COLE AND DO MY JOB.

NEXT TIME, EXPLODE INTO HIM.

USE YOUR HANDS AND FOREARMS TO FORCE HIM INTO WHICHEVER DIRECTION YOU NEED.

I WAS **SHOCKED**. THEY ACTUALLY WANTED TO HELP ME! I SUDDENLY FELT A NEW BURST OF ENERGY.

LIKE THIS?

YEAH, EXACTLY, JUST LIKE THAT!

OKAY, I THINK I GOT IT. THANKS, MAX.

HIKE!

BOOYAH! BLOCKED YA!

OKAY, MAYBE I GOT A LITTLE TOO EXCITED, BUT IT FELT GREAT TO **NOT** GET KNOCKED ON MY BUTT FOR ONCE THIS PRACTICE.

PLUS, EVEN MAX WAS BEING NICE!

I REALLY WISHED BREE WAS THERE TODAY.

BUT I GUESS I NEEDED TO GET USED TO HER NOT BEING AROUND.

AND HONESTLY, NOW I FELT LIKE MAYBE I COULD.

AFTER PRACTICE, MY WHOLE "TACKLING MAKING FRIENDS" PLAN SUDDENLY SEEMED HARDER THAN I THOUGHT IT'D BE...

YEAH! WE WERE JUST TALKING ABOUT GOING ICE-SKATING NEXT WEEKEND.

WANT TO GO WITH US?

WE'VE NEVER GONE BEFORE, SO IT SHOULD BE... INTERESTING.

SURE! I'VE NEVER BEEN ICE-SKATING BEFORE, EITHER.

COOL!

WE'RE HOPING SOME CUTE BOYS WILL BE THERE.

NO, **YOU'RE** HOPING CUTE BOYS WILL BE THERE. I'M HOPING TO DISCOVER MY TRUE CALLING AS AN OLYMPIC FIGURE SKATER.

YES! OLYMPICS, HERE WE COME!

I HAD A NEW POSITION AND I WAS MAKING NEW FRIENDS. NOW IT WAS TIME FOR MY BRAND-NEW LOOK. I COULDN'T WAIT!

I WAS SO STOKED WHEN MOM VOLUNTEERED TO HELP ME WITH MY MAKEOVER.

IT WAS THE FIRST TIME WE'D DONE ANYTHING TOGETHER— JUST THE TWO OF US—IN FOREVER. (WELL, SINCE THE TWINS WERE BORN, ANYWAY.)

I REALLY MISSED IT.

I CAN'T BELIEVE I'M LETTING YOU DO THIS...

IT'S TOO LATE TO CHANGE YOUR MIND NOW, MOM.

MANIAC BLEACH 9.77

MANIAC BLEACH

I KNOW, BUT IT'S SO HARD TO KEEP UP WITH BLOND HAIR. YOU REALIZE THAT, RIGHT?

YEAH, YEAH... STOP WORRYING, IT'LL BE FINE.

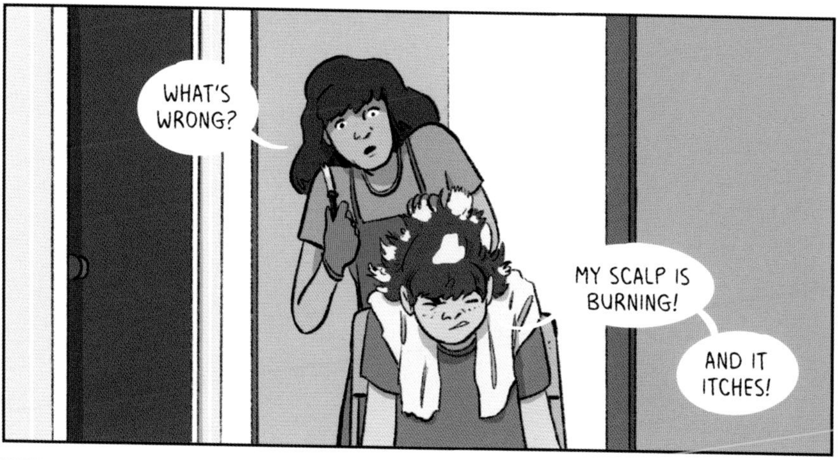
WHAT'S WRONG?
MY SCALP IS BURNING!
AND IT ITCHES!

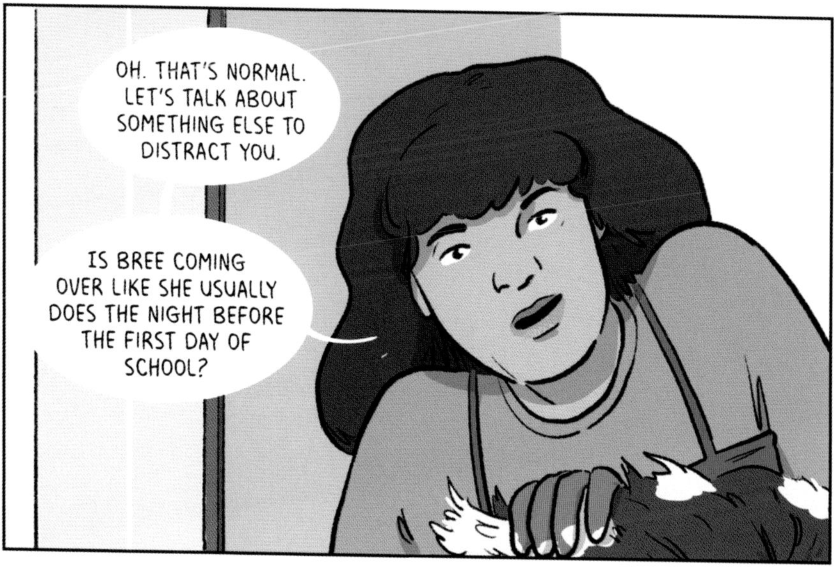
OH. THAT'S NORMAL. LET'S TALK ABOUT SOMETHING ELSE TO DISTRACT YOU.
IS BREE COMING OVER LIKE SHE USUALLY DOES THE NIGHT BEFORE THE FIRST DAY OF SCHOOL?

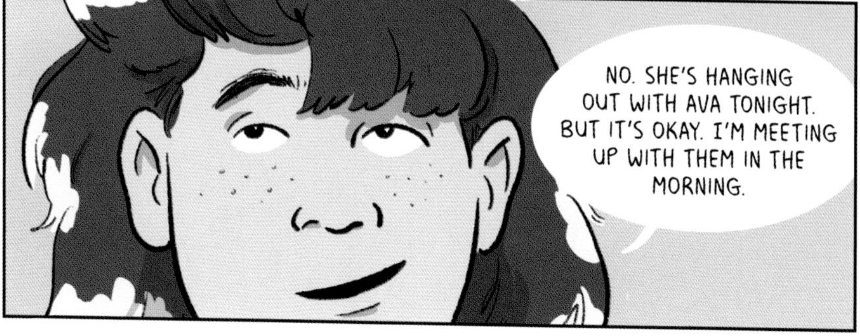
NO. SHE'S HANGING OUT WITH AVA TONIGHT. BUT IT'S OKAY. I'M MEETING UP WITH THEM IN THE MORNING.

AND I'M ACTUALLY PRETTY EXCITED THAT MY WHOLE MAKEOVER WILL BE A SURPRISE.

I'M GLAD YOU'RE EXCITED. I REALLY AM. BUT I HOPE YOU AREN'T CHANGING FOR OTHER PEOPLE...

I KNOW, I KNOW.

THIS IS WHAT I WANT.

I'M GONNA LOOK AMAZING.

ALL RIGHT... WELL, ARE YOU READY FOR THESE, THEN?

SURE, IT CAN'T BE **THAT** BAD, RIGHT?

RIGHT. IF YOU CAN HANDLE FOOTBALL, YOU CAN HANDLE GETTING YOUR EYEBROWS PLUCKED.

OF COURSE I COULD...

PLUCK

...ESPECIALLY IF IT MEANT FITTING IN WITH AVA.

AS THE SAYING GOES: *NO PAIN, NO GAIN!*

CHAPTER 5

ON MONDAY MORNING, MY STOMACH WAS DOING SOMERSAULTS.

HEADING TO SCHOOL! BYE, MOM!

BYE! HAVE FUN!

WOW! YOU LOOK SO PRETTY!

THANKS, LIV.

I WAS **SO EXCITED** FOR THE FIRST DAY OF SEVENTH GRADE.

UHHH...

THE OTHER KIDS DEFINITELY SEEMED SURPRISED...

...BUT NOT NECESSARILY IN A GOOD WAY...

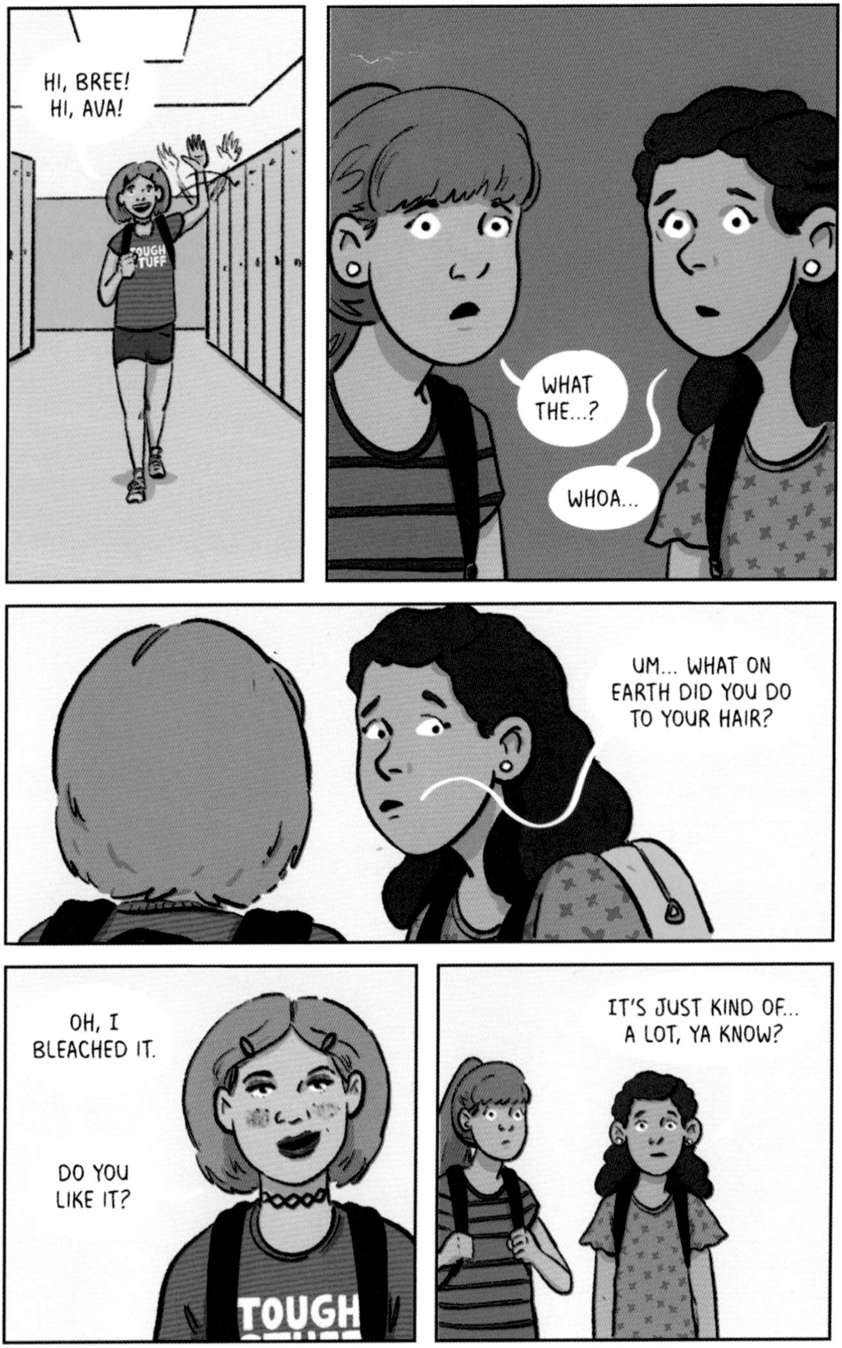
HI, BREE!
HI, AVA!
TOUGH STUFF
WHAT THE...?
WHOA...
UM... WHAT ON EARTH DID YOU DO TO YOUR HAIR?
OH, I BLEACHED IT.
DO YOU LIKE IT?
TOUGH
IT'S JUST KIND OF... A LOT, YA KNOW?

YEAH, I WASN'T SURE HOW I FELT ABOUT IT AT FIRST, BUT I THINK I REALLY LIKE IT!

RRRIIINNNGG

WE SHOULD PROBABLY GO FIND OUR LOCKERS...

BREE AND AVA HADN'T EXACTLY HAD THE REACTION I'D EXPECTED...

WERE WE NOT SEEING THE SAME THING? I THOUGHT I LOOKED GOOD...

BUT NOW I WASN'T SO SURE.

WHAT'S WRONG WITH YOUR EYES? DID YOU GET PUNCHED IN THE FACE OR SOMETHING?

IT'S MAKEUP, FART BREATH!

UGH.

I **DID** LOOK A LOT DIFFERENT. MAYBE EVERYONE WAS JUST USED TO SPORTY MISTY. MAYBE THEY JUST NEEDED TIME TO THINK OF ME AS **CUTE** AND **GIRLY**.

STILL, I WAS FEELING A LITTLE SELF-CONSCIOUS.

BY THE TIME LUNCH ROLLED AROUND, KIDS SEEMED TO HAVE STOPPED WHISPERING ABOUT ME, SO THINGS WERE LOOKING UP. AND NOW I GOT TO SIT AT THE **POPULAR KID TABLE!**

HI, EVERYONE!

YOU ARE NEVER GONNA BELIEVE WHAT MAX ASKED ME IN SCIENCE TODAY! IT WAS SO RUDE—

YOU KNOW, YOU HAVE LIPSTICK OR BLOOD OR SOMETHING ON YOUR TEETH...

HEE-HEE.

HEE-HEE.

HEE-HEE.

HEE-HEE.

I'LL BE RIGHT BACK.

I WAS GLAD AVA POINTED IT OUT SO I WASN'T WALKING AROUND WITH RED TEETH THE REST OF THE DAY...

...BUT DID SHE REALLY HAVE TO DO IT IN FRONT OF **EVERYBODY**?

I WILL NOT CRY.
I WILL NOT CRY.
I WILL NOT CRY.

TOUGH STUFF

HEY, MISTY. WE SAW YOU PRACTICALLY SPRINT OUT OF THE CAFETERIA.

ARE YOU OKAY?

YES.

NO.

AVA JUST POINTED OUT THAT I HAD LIPSTICK ON MY TEETH—IN FRONT OF THE WHOLE TABLE!

YEAH, WE OVERHEARD. IT WAS PRETTY MESSED UP.

BUT IT'LL BE OKAY!

LOOK, NOW THAT YOU HAVE BLOND HAIR—WHICH I **LOVE**—YOU DON'T NEED SUCH DARK LIPSTICK.

HERE, YOU CAN USE MY CLEAR LIP GLOSS. IT'LL BE PERFECT.

AND YOUR EYESHADOW IS A LITTLE SMUDGED, SO YOU MIGHT WANT TO WIPE SOME OFF.

UGH. I CAN'T BELIEVE I WAS WALKING AROUND ALL MORNING LOOKING LIKE A DERANGED VAMPIRE CLOWN!

HEY, WE'VE ALL BEEN THERE.

I LOVE YOUR SHIRT, BY THE WAY. IT'S VERY YOU.

THANKS!

WOW. I DID LOOK BETTER, AND I FELT A LOT MORE LIKE MYSELF.

TOUGH

YOU'RE THE BEST. I OWE YOU A CHOCOLATE MILK AT LUNCH ONE DAY.

HA-HA! OKAY!

WELL, THANKS AGAIN! I BETTER GET BACK BEFORE THEY THINK I FELL IN THE TOILET OR SOMETHING.

OKAY... WELL, GOOD LUCK OVER THERE...

OH, GOOD, MISTY, THAT'S SO MUCH BETTER.

YEAH! YOU LOOK NORMAL NOW.

YEAH...

THANKS...

IF BREE COULD FIT IN WITH THE POPULAR GIRLS, SO COULD I. JUST LIKE AT FOOTBALL, I WAS GONNA HAVE TO TRY HARDER.

BY THE END OF THE FIRST WEEK OF SCHOOL, I'D **MOSTLY** PERFECTED MY NEW LOOK. ALL IT TOOK WAS LESS MAKEUP AND FEWER HAIR ACCESSORIES...

...AND ACCEPTING THAT I'D PROBABLY ALWAYS HATE MY NEW CLOTHES.

PLUS, I REALLY COULDN'T STAND WEARING CONTACTS ALL DAY.

ONCE EVERYONE GOT USED TO MY BLOND HAIR, I WAS ABLE TO START FOCUSING ON MY FIRST FOOTBALL GAME—AND IT WAS **FINALLY** HERE.

SOME PEOPLE GET BUTTERFLIES IN THEIR STOMACH WHEN THEY GET NERVOUS, OR THEIR KNEES SHAKE A LOT, BUT ME? I ALWAYS GOT SUPER NAUSEOUS.

AND COACH G HAD PUT ME IN THE STARTING LINEUP, WHICH WAS SUPER-COOL, BUT TALK ABOUT PRESSURE!

I WAS GLAD CRAIG WAS THERE. I JUST REALLY WISHED MOM COULD HAVE COME, TOO.

BUT, OF COURSE, THE TWINS COULDN'T MISS THEIR NAP.

ARE YOU OKAY? YOU DON'T LOOK SO GREAT...

YEAH, I'M FINE.

I HOPE...

FORTY-FOUR DRIVE!
LET'S DO THIS!

MISTY!

ME?!

YES, YOU!

I **NEED** YOU TO MAKE SURE THAT HOLE IS OPEN!

THE PLAY WAS RESTING ON MY SHOULDERS.

NO BIG DEAL, RIGHT?

BREAK!

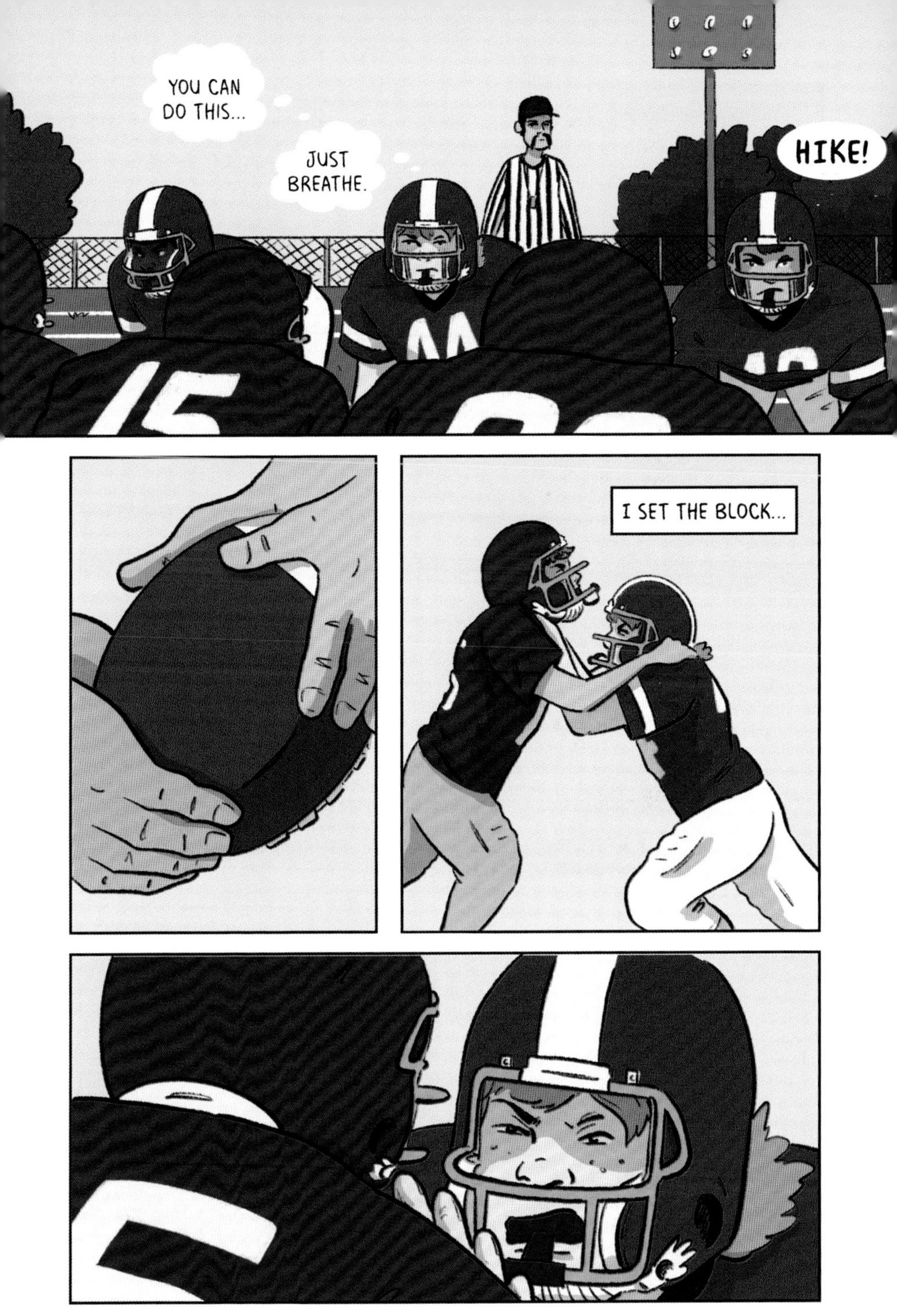
YOU CAN DO THIS...
JUST BREATHE.
HIKE!
I SET THE BLOCK...

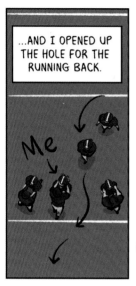

...AND I OPENED UP THE HOLE FOR THE RUNNING BACK.

Me

BUT MY DEFENDER WAS STRONG, AND I COULDN'T STAY ON MY FEET FOR LONG.

SLAM

TOUCHDOWN!

HOLY MOLY! WE DID IT. THAT WAS AWESOME!

TOUCHDOWN!

YES!

SIX POINTS ON THE BOARD!

YES!

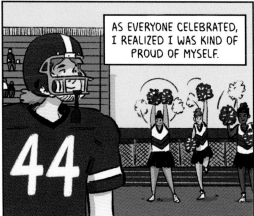

AS EVERYONE CELEBRATED, I REALIZED I WAS KIND OF PROUD OF MYSELF.

GOOD BLOCK, MISTY!

WAY TO OPEN THE HOLE!

THE GAME WENT ON...

...AND THE NERVES AND THE SICK FEELING FROM EARLIER WENT AWAY.

ONE THING WAS FOR SURE: THE FOOTBALL FIELD WAS **EXACTLY** WHERE I WAS MEANT TO BE.

GOOD GAME.

GOOD GAME.

GOOD GAME.

GOOD GAME.

GOOD GAME.

GOOD GAME.

WAIT...

YOU'RE A GIRL?

DUDE, YOU HIT HARDER THAN MOST OF THE GUYS I PLAY AGAINST...

IT WAS THE BEST COMPLIMENT EVER.

THAT WAS SO COOL!

OUR TEAM IS REALLY GOOD THIS SEASON!

GOOD GAME, MISTY!

THANKS, CHARLIE! YOU TOO. AND, NICK, THAT WAS AN AWESOME TOUCHDOWN OUT THERE.

HMPH. WHATEVER.

NICK DIDN'T WANT TO ACCEPT ME AS A TEAMMATE NOW, BUT I FIGURED I'D WIN HIM OVER, ONE COMPLIMENT AT A TIME. (PLUS, IT **WAS** A GREAT TOUCHDOWN.)

MISTY! THAT WAS PHENOMENAL!

I CAN'T WAIT TO TELL YOUR MOM ABOUT IT. WAY TO BE AGGRESSIVE!

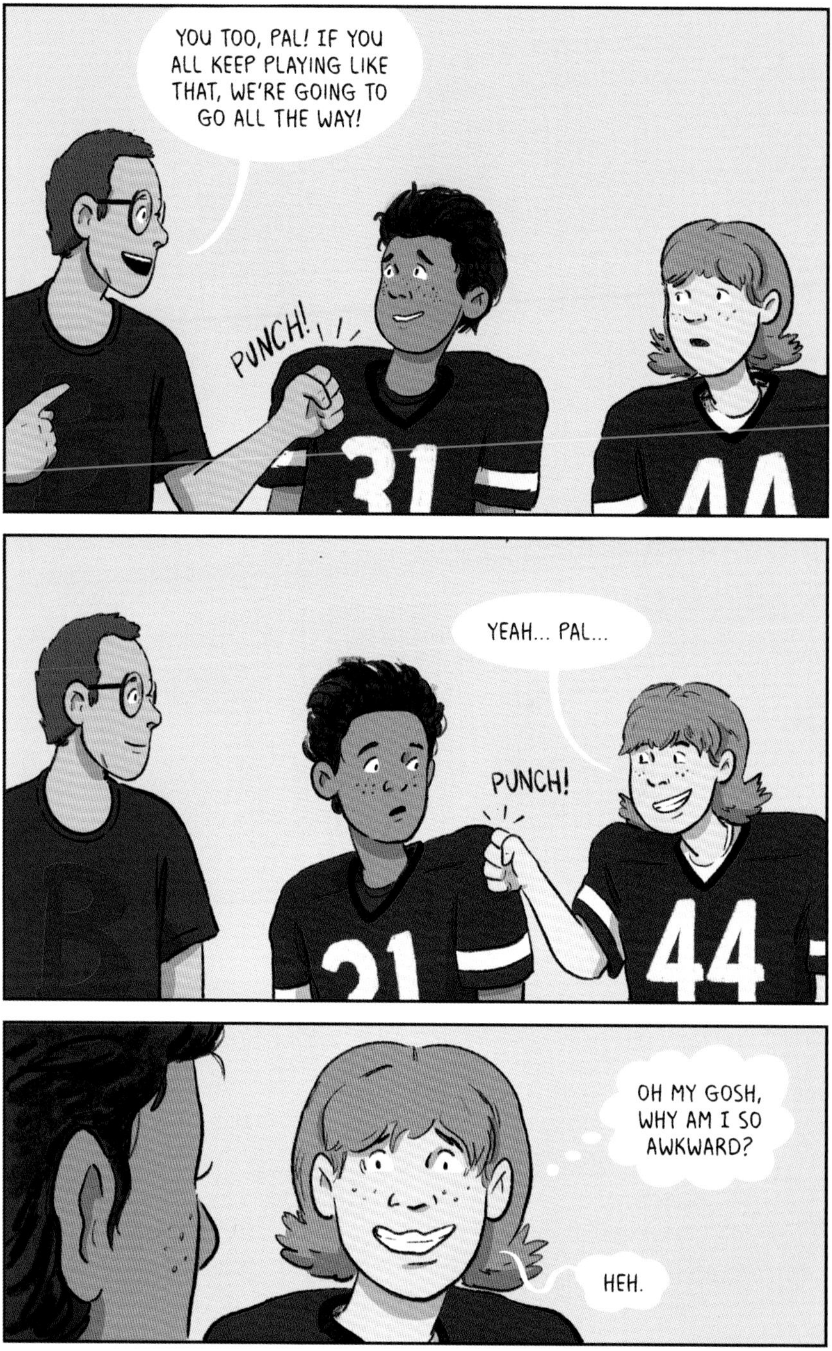
YOU TOO, PAL! IF YOU ALL KEEP PLAYING LIKE THAT, WE'RE GOING TO GO ALL THE WAY!
PUNCH!
YEAH... PAL...
PUNCH!
OH MY GOSH, WHY AM I SO AWKWARD?
HEH.

SO, ARE WE STILL GOING ICE-SKATING TOMORROW?

SEE YA!

FOR SURE!

MY MOM SAYS WE'RE ALL GOING TO LEAVE WITH BRUISED BUTTS FROM FALLING!

NAH. I'M REALLY GOOD AT ROLLERBLADING. IT'S PROBABLY THE SAME.

HMMM... DO YOU THINK I COULD GET OUT OF PE ON MONDAY IF I HAVE A BRUISED BUTT...?

YOU KNOW, I USED TO PLAY HOCKEY IN A MEN'S LEAGUE. I COULD COME AND GIVE YOU GIRLS SOME POINTERS.

UH... NO THANK YOU...

HOW HARD COULD IT BE?

THE NEXT AFTERNOON, MOM DROPPED ME OFF AT THE ICE RINK WITH JENNA AND AMANDA.

IT WAS SUPER EASY TO HANG OUT WITH THEM. I'D TOTALLY FORGOTTEN WHAT IT WAS LIKE TO JUST RELAX AND HAVE FUN OFF THE FOOTBALL FIELD.

ICE ARENA

CAN I COME WITH YOU? PLEEAAASSSEEE?

MAYBE NEXT TIME.

I CAN'T WAIT TO DO A TRIPLE AXEL!

DO YOU EVEN KNOW WHAT A TRIPLE AXEL IS?

HERE GOES NOTHING...

SWOOP

ARE YOU OKAY?!

YEAH. I GUESS IT'S NOT LIKE ROLLERBLADING.

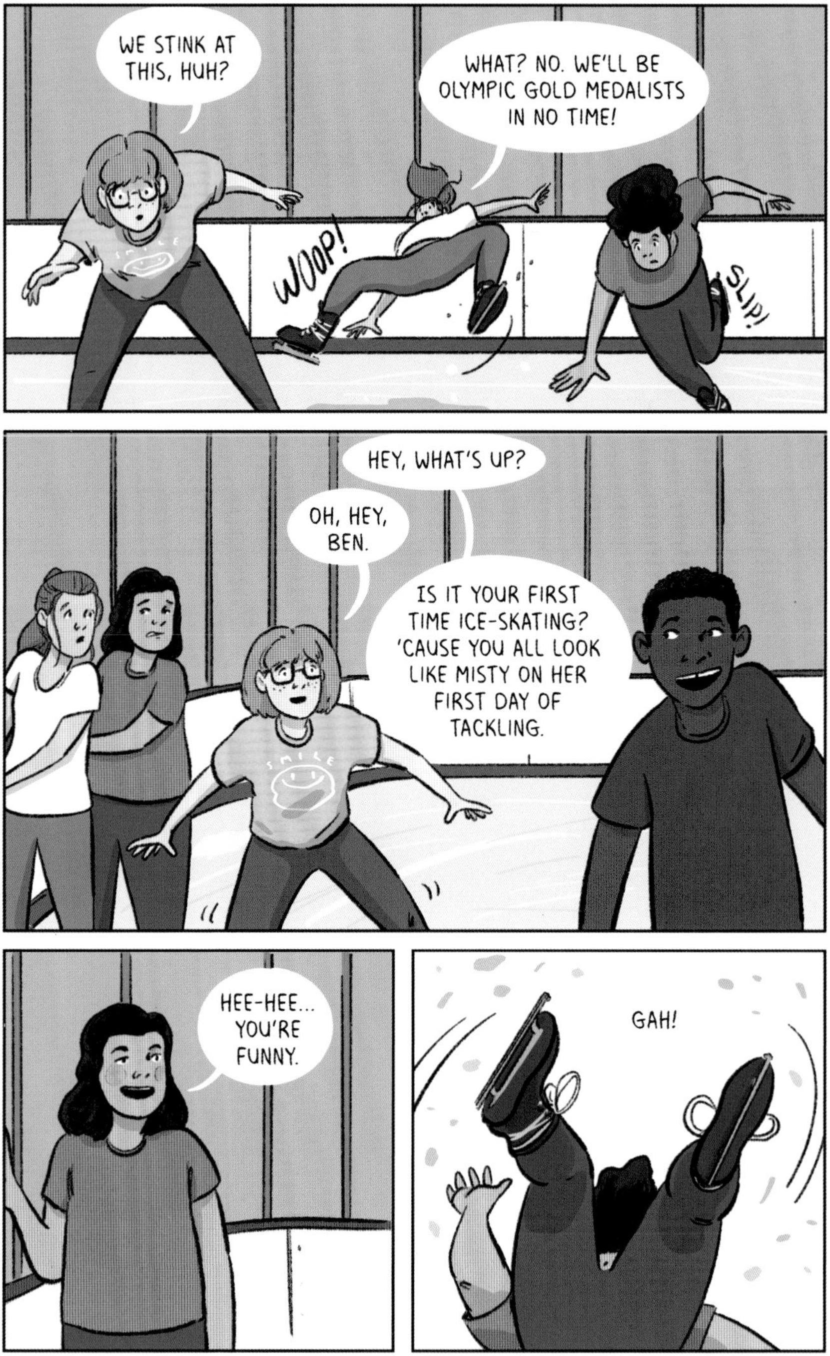
WE STINK AT THIS, HUH?
WHAT? NO. WE'LL BE OLYMPIC GOLD MEDALISTS IN NO TIME!
WOOP!
SLIP!
HEY, WHAT'S UP?
OH, HEY, BEN.
IS IT YOUR FIRST TIME ICE-SKATING? 'CAUSE YOU ALL LOOK LIKE MISTY ON HER FIRST DAY OF TACKLING.
HEE-HEE... YOU'RE FUNNY.
GAH!

HA-HA... YOU KNOW, IF I COULD SKATE BETTER, I'D TACKLE YOU RIGHT NOW.

WELP, GUESS I'M LUCKY YOU CAN'T, THEN, HUH?

ANYWAY, I HAVE TO GET BACK TO MY LITTLE BROTHER'S BIRTHDAY PARTY.

HAVE FUN! SEE YA LATER.

WOW, AMANDA, THAT WAS **SMOOTH**...

UGH...

THAT'S RIGHT. I FORGOT YOU LIKE BEN.

PLEASE DON'T TELL HIM!

MY LIPS ARE ZIPPED.

AMANDA WAS OBVIOUSLY JUST AS SHY AS I WAS WHEN IT CAME TO CRUSHES. IT SORT OF MADE ME FEEL BETTER ABOUT BEING SO AWKWARD AROUND CHARLIE ALL THE TIME.

SO, WHAT'S BREE UP TO THIS WEEKEND?

NOT SURE. PROBABLY HANGING OUT WITH AVA.

BREE AND I BARELY TALKED ALL WEEK. WE HAD SOME CLASSES TOGETHER AND WE ATE LUNCH TOGETHER, BUT THINGS WERE DEFINITELY... DIFFERENT.

YEAH, IT'S STRANGE. I KNEW YOU AND AVA WERE ON THE BASKETBALL TEAM TOGETHER, BUT I DIDN'T REALIZE YOU WERE FRIENDS.

YEAH, WE STARTED HANGING OUT AT THE END OF SUMMER.

THAT'S COOL. AVA'S... NICE...

YEAH, IF IT'S OPPOSITE DAY!

SHE'S SORT OF LIKE AN ONION—THE LONGER YOU'RE AROUND HER, THE MORE LIKELY YOU ARE TO CRY...

HA-HA-HA!

HA-HA-HA!

I FELT A LITTLE BETTER KNOWING OTHER PEOPLE SAW WHAT I WAS STARTING TO SEE—THAT AVA WASN'T PERFECT.

YET, FOR SOME REASON, IT STILL BOTHERED ME THAT SHE WAS FRIENDS WITH BREE BUT NOT **ME**.

FOR SOME REASON, I STILL WANTED HER TO ACCEPT ME.

CHAPTER 6

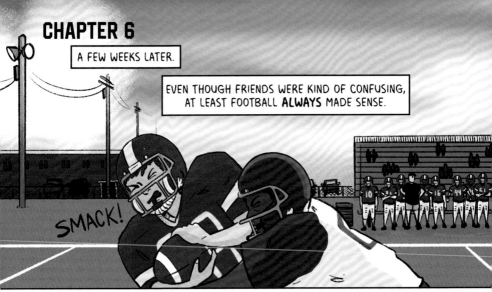

A FEW WEEKS LATER.

EVEN THOUGH FRIENDS WERE KIND OF CONFUSING, AT LEAST FOOTBALL **ALWAYS** MADE SENSE.

SMACK!

NICK, GET IN THERE.

GO GET 'EM, NICK!

BUT MY TEAM WAS PLAYING THE TOUGHEST GAME OF THE SEASON SO FAR, AGAINST PLAYERS WHO SEEMED TO GET ANGRIER EVERY TIME WE SCORED.

SMACK!

DANG!

THE KID I WAS BLOCKING WAS A BEAST.

HE WAS BIGGER AND STRONGER THAN ME, AND HE WAS EVEN MEANER THAN COLE.

I COULDN'T WAIT FOR THE GAME TO BE OVER.

THAT'S THE GAME!

A GIRL PLAYING FOOTBALL... WHAT A JOKE.

WHAT THE—

HEY!

ARE YOU SERIOUS?

AW, HOW CUTE, STICKING UP FOR YOUR LITTLE GIRLFRIEND.

GIRLFRIEND?

ARE YOU OKAY?

YEAH, I'M FINE. THANKS.

WE'RE ALL GOING FOR PIZZA AT MARIO'S IF YOU WANT TO COME.

REALLY?! HECK YEAH!

THEY **DO** HAVE THEIR FAMOUS POPCORN-FLAVORED ICE CREAM...

YUCK, THAT STUFF IS GROSS.

WHAT?! **YOU'RE** GROSS!

...JUST KIDDING...

OH, YOU'RE COMING THIS TIME, MISTY?

YEP...

THAT'S COOL.

IT IS?

ARE YOU SURE YOU DON'T WANT ANY?

EW, NO THANKS.

I'LL TAKE SOME! I LOVE THE BUTTER FLAVOR!

I DON'T KNOW, NICK. YOU SHOULD BE CAREFUL—YOU ALREADY HAD BUTTERFINGERS OUT THERE TODAY.

OOHHHH! BURN!!!

OKAY, FINE... THAT WAS A GOOD ONE...

IT WAS PRETTY INCREDIBLE TO FINALLY FEEL LIKE I BELONGED.

AS EASY AND AS FUN AS IT WAS WITH THE BOYS, THE NEXT DAY AT SCHOOL WAS BASICALLY THE OPPOSITE.

BUT IF THERE WAS ONE THING I'D LEARNED FROM FOOTBALL, IT WAS THAT SOMETIMES IT JUST TAKES PEOPLE A WHILE TO COME AROUND.

I HATE PE.

ME TOO.

OH... UH... ME TOO.

I'M SO TIRED.

I KNOW. I CAN HARDLY BREATHE!

YEAH. I'M DYING OVER HERE...

IT ISN'T FAIR THAT WE HAVE TO GET ALL SWEATY AND GROSS THEN GO TO CLASS.

YEAH, I WISH I WENT TO AN ALL-GIRLS SCHOOL SO BOYS WOULDN'T SMELL ME AFTER THIS.

UGH. SAME!

WHAT?

BOYS SEE YOU LOOKING LIKE THIS ALL THE TIME AT FOOTBALL.

AND WHY DO YOU CARE? YOU DON'T EVEN LIKE BOYS.

WWHHEEEEEEEE

I... UM...

SAVED BY THE BELL... OR THE WHISTLE, I GUESS.

LADIES! THIS ISN'T SOCIAL HOUR! START YOUR SCRIMMAGE!

BRICK

BOX HER
OUT!

HUH?

GOT
IT.

BLOCK!

IN YOUR FACE!

WHATEVER.

I'M GOING TO THE BATHROOM.

WHY'D YOU DO THAT?

WHAT?

I WAS JUST PLAYING AROUND.

FINE. MAYBE I WENT A LITTLE OVERBOARD. I'LL SAY SORRY.

ANYWAY, I HAVE A GAME SATURDAY. YOU WANNA COME? I WAS THINKING YOU COULD SLEEP OVER AFTERWARD.

OH. SORRY, I CAN'T... I'M GOING BOWLING WITH AVA'S FAMILY SATURDAY NIGHT.

OKAY.

145

BUT SHE'S SLEEPING OVER FRIDAY NIGHT. YOU CAN SPEND THE NIGHT, TOO, IF YOU WANT...

OH... I GUESS THAT COULD BE FUN.

FOR SURE.

LADIES! STOP! CHATTING!

UGH. FINE...

MAYBE A SLEEPOVER WITH AVA WASN'T A BAD IDEA. I NEEDED TO HANG OUT WITH HER OUTSIDE OF SCHOOL MORE SO SHE COULD SEE THAT I COULD BE COOL, TOO.

AND MAYBE THEN SHE AND BREE WOULD BE A LITTLE NICER.

I'D BEEN SO DISTRACTED LATELY, BETWEEN FOOTBALL, BREE AND AVA, AND THE SLEEPOVER, THAT I'D COMPLETELY FORGOTTEN ABOUT THE OTHER EXCITING EVENT COMING UP...

Are you going to the dance next week?

Obviously! I Gotta show off my dance moves!

RIIINNGGG!!

I CAN'T WAIT TO SEE THEM!

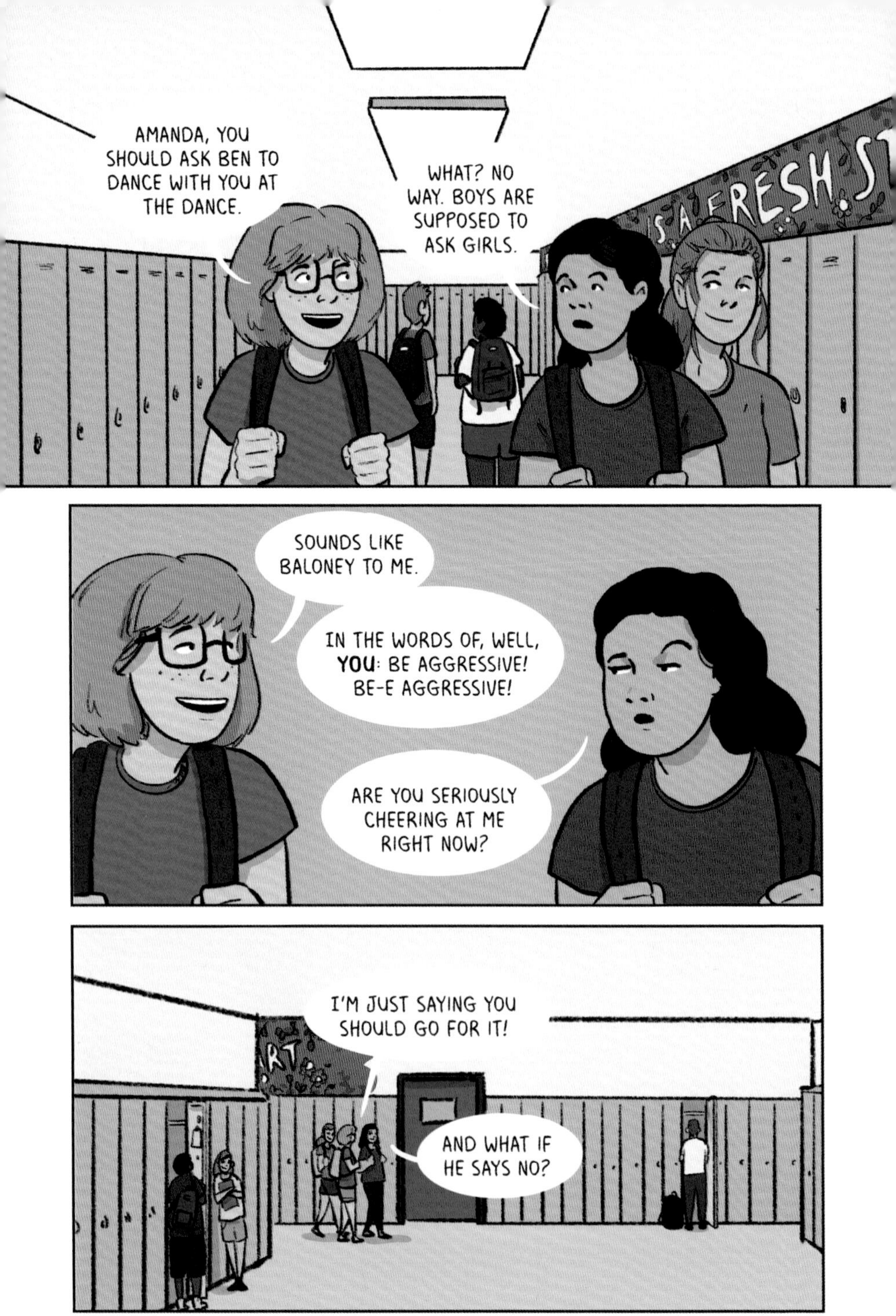
AMANDA, YOU SHOULD ASK BEN TO DANCE WITH YOU AT THE DANCE.
WHAT? NO WAY. BOYS ARE SUPPOSED TO ASK GIRLS.
IS A FRESH ST
SOUNDS LIKE BALONEY TO ME.
IN THE WORDS OF, WELL, **YOU**: BE AGGRESSIVE! BE-E AGGRESSIVE!
ARE YOU SERIOUSLY CHEERING AT ME RIGHT NOW?
I'M JUST SAYING YOU SHOULD GO FOR IT!
AND WHAT IF HE SAYS NO?

WELL, YOU KNOW, WHEN YOU GET KNOCKED DOWN, YOU JUST HAVE TO GET BACK UP AGAIN.

OH, OKAY, COACH. SHOULD I TACKLE HIM WHEN I ASK, TOO?

MAYBE I WASN'T THE BEST PERSON TO GIVE BOY ADVICE. I WOULDN'T EVEN TELL ANYONE I LIKED CHARLIE, MUCH LESS ASK HIM TO DANCE WITH ME.

HMMM... MAYBE IF HE SAYS NO.

HA-HA!

HA-HA!

BUT I DID FEEL WAY MORE COMFORTABLE TALKING TO JENNA AND AMANDA ABOUT BOY STUFF THAN I DID TALKING TO BREE.

STILL, I WASN'T READY TO TELL THEM ABOUT CHARLIE.

I GUESS YOU PROBABLY SHOULDN'T LISTEN TO ME. I ONLY EVER DANCED WITH BREE AT THE DANCES LAST YEAR.

IF YOU WANT, YOU CAN COME TO THE DANCE WITH AMANDA AND ME. HER DAD'S GOING TO DRIVE US.

SURE. THAT'D BE FUN!

WHO KNEW, MAYBE I'D BE ABLE TO WORK UP THE COURAGE TO ASK CHARLIE TO DANCE WITH ME BY THEN.

CENTRAL MIDDLE SCHOOL

BUT PROBABLY NOT.

BREE'S SLEEPOVER WAS TOMORROW. I WAS EXCITED, BUT STILL, IT WAS HARD TO FORGET HOW RUDE AVA AND BREE WERE WHEN THEY WERE TOGETHER.

LISTEN UP, BEARS! THIS WEEKEND IS OUR LAST REGULAR SEASON GAME, AND AS AN UNDEFEATED TEAM, WE'RE GUARANTEED A SPOT IN THE PLAYOFFS.

I WAS HAVING A REALLY HARD TIME FOCUSING ON PRACTICE.

SO, I'VE DECIDED TO SWITCH IT UP AND HAVE SOME PLAYERS TRY DIFFERENT POSITIONS TODAY.

WE'LL SEE HOW IT GOES, THEN MAYBE WE'LL TRY IT OUT IN SATURDAY'S GAME.

NEVER MIND. I WAS DEFINITELY PAYING ATTENTION NOW.

HEY, MAYBE YOU'LL FINALLY GET TO TRY OUT DEFENSE.

I HOPE SO!

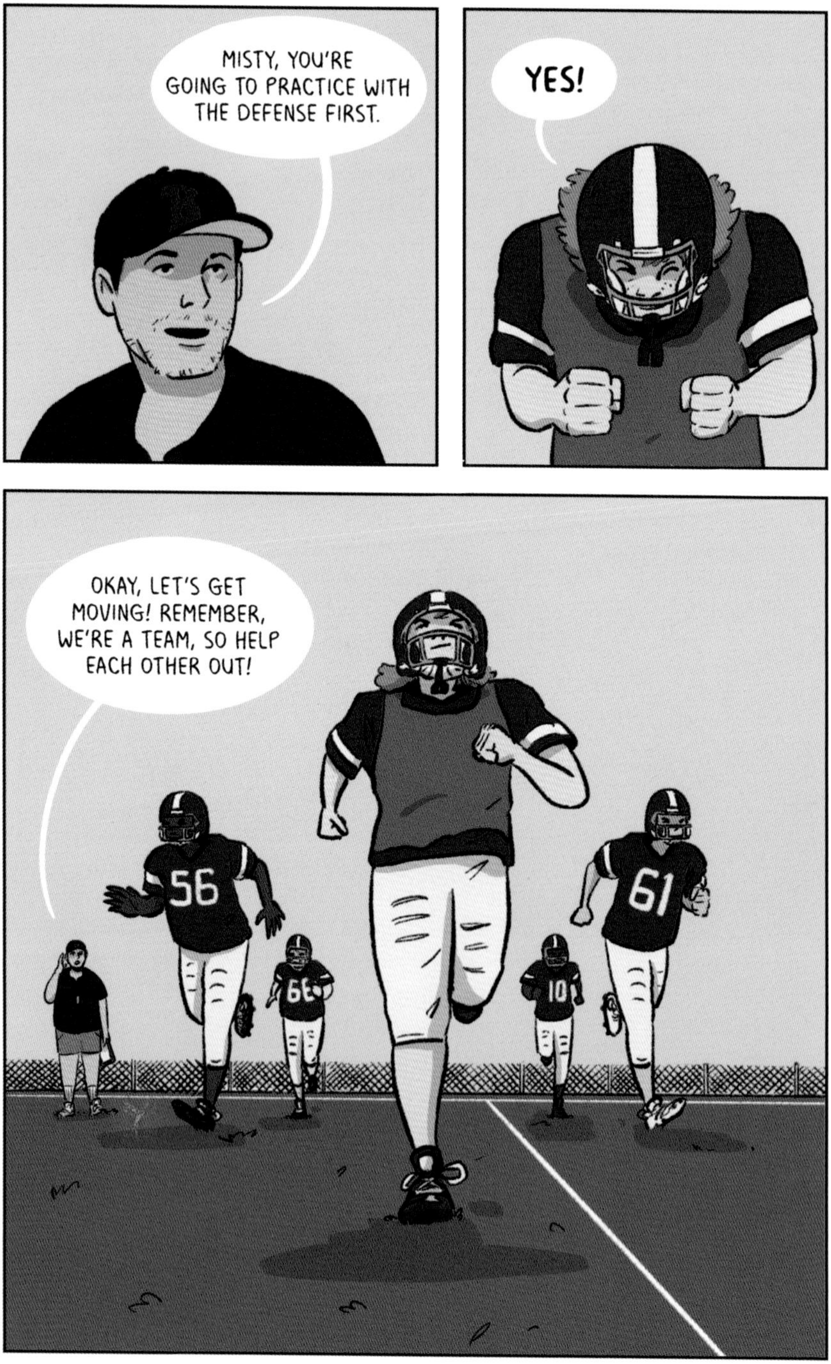
MISTY, YOU'RE GOING TO PRACTICE WITH THE DEFENSE FIRST.
YES!
OKAY, LET'S GET MOVING! REMEMBER, WE'RE A TEAM, SO HELP EACH OTHER OUT!
56
61
66
10

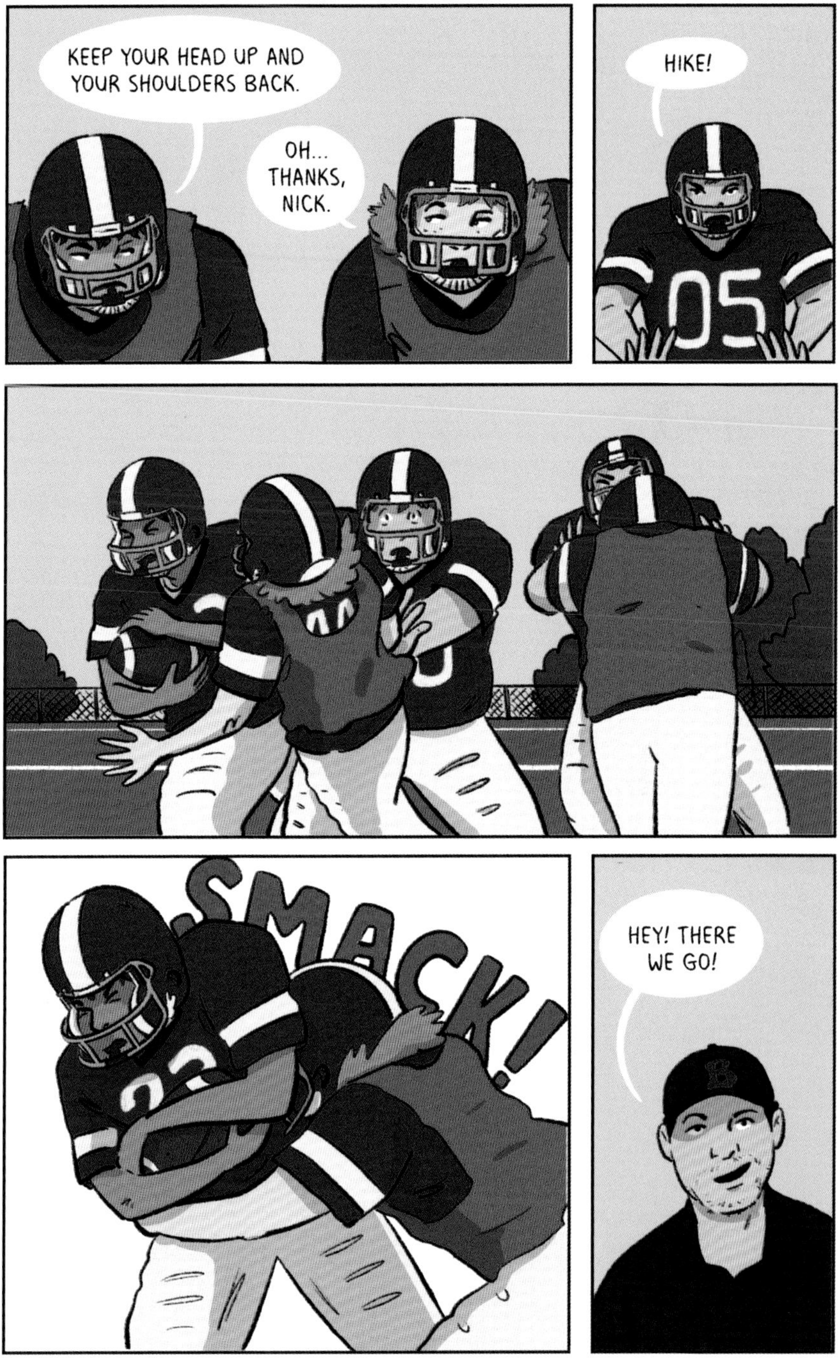
KEEP YOUR HEAD UP AND YOUR SHOULDERS BACK.
OH... THANKS, NICK.
HIKE!
05
SMACK!
HEY! THERE WE GO!

MISTY, YOU'RE DOING GREAT!

YOU KNOW WHAT? I WANT TO SEE HOW YOU DO AT HALFBACK.

REALLY?

HALFBACK IS AN OFFENSIVE POSITION. THEY CARRY THE BALL ON MOST RUNNING PLAYS.

BOYS, WHY DON'T YOU HELP MISTY PRACTICE HANDOFFS?

A HANDOFF IS WHEN THE BALL IS HANDED TO SOMEONE BY A TEAMMATE, TYPICALLY TO RUN IT TO THE END ZONE TO SCORE A TOUCHDOWN.

I COULDN'T BELIEVE I MIGHT GET A CHANCE TO PUT SOME POINTS ON THE BOARD!

HIKE!

IF ONLY I COULD STOP FUMBLING THE BALL WHEN IT WAS HANDED TO ME.

DANG IT!

I DON'T KNOW WHY I CAN'T HOLD ON TO IT.

BECAUSE YOU'RE GRABBING FOR IT.

WHEN YOU RUN UP FOR THE HANDOFF...

...MAKE SURE YOUR ARMS ARE LIKE THIS.

THEN THE QUARTERBACK CAN PLACE THE BALL IN THERE, AND YOU JUST TUCK IT AND RUN.

WHY ARE YOU HELPING HER, CHARLIE? IT'S ALMOST LIKE YOU ACTUALLY **WANT** HER ON THE TEAM.

JEEZ. JUST CUT IT OUT ALREADY, COLE. YOUR ATTITUDE IS GETTING OLD.

CHARLIE WAS PROBABLY JUST TIRED OF LISTENING TO COLE, BUT STILL, HE'D YELLED AT HIM FOR ME. IT WAS KIND OF A BIG DEAL.

YOU KNOW, I CAN HANDLE HIM MYSELF. I'M PRETTY GOOD AT JUST IGNORING HIM.

I KNOW, BUT TEAMMATES ARE SUPPOSED TO HAVE YOUR BACK. PLUS, FRIENDS DON'T LET PEOPLE TREAT THEIR FRIENDS LIKE THAT.

YOU SHOULD TELL COACH G, THOUGH.

THAT WOULD JUST MAKE COLE HATE ME MORE. BESIDES, HE'LL COME AROUND, EVEN IF IT TAKES ALL SEASON.

OKAY... IF YOU SAY SO.

I WAS DETERMINED TO SHOW COLE THAT I DESERVED TO BE ON THE TEAM—NO MATTER HOW MEAN HE WAS TO ME.

YOU READY TO TRY AGAIN?

I THINK SO?

COOL. LET'S DO IT.

HIKE!

WITH CHARLIE'S HELP AND A LOT MORE PRACTICE, I GOT THE HANG OF HANDOFFS AND RUNNING THE BALL.

I FELT **UNSTOPPABLE**.

CHAPTER 7

FINALLY, IT WAS TIME FOR THE SLEEPOVER. I'D BEEN PRETTY EXCITED ALL DAY, BUT WHEN BREE AND AVA ANSWERED THE DOOR, I SUDDENLY FELT LIKE I DIDN'T BELONG THERE.

HEY, MISTY!

HI.

WE WERE JUST ABOUT TO MAKE ICE-CREAM SUNDAES AND WATCH A MOVIE.

I LIKE YOUR... PAJAMAS.

THAT'S WHEN I NOTICED THEY WERE WEARING MATCHING PAJAMAS.

I DIDN'T WANT TO CARE. BUT I WISHED I HAD GOTTEN THE MEMO ABOUT THE RIDICULOUS PICKLE PAJAMAS.

THANKS.

YOU TWO LOOK CUTE.

OKAY, LET'S GO WATCH THE MOVIE. I CALL DIBS ON THE COUCH—WITH BREE!

WE'RE GOING TO WATCH MY FAVORITE MOVIE—*DIRTY DANCING*!

I LOVE PATRICK SWAYZE. HE'S SO DREAMY.

OH MY GOSH. YES, HE IS!

WHO IS PATRICK SWAYZE?

OH, YEAH, SO CUTE!

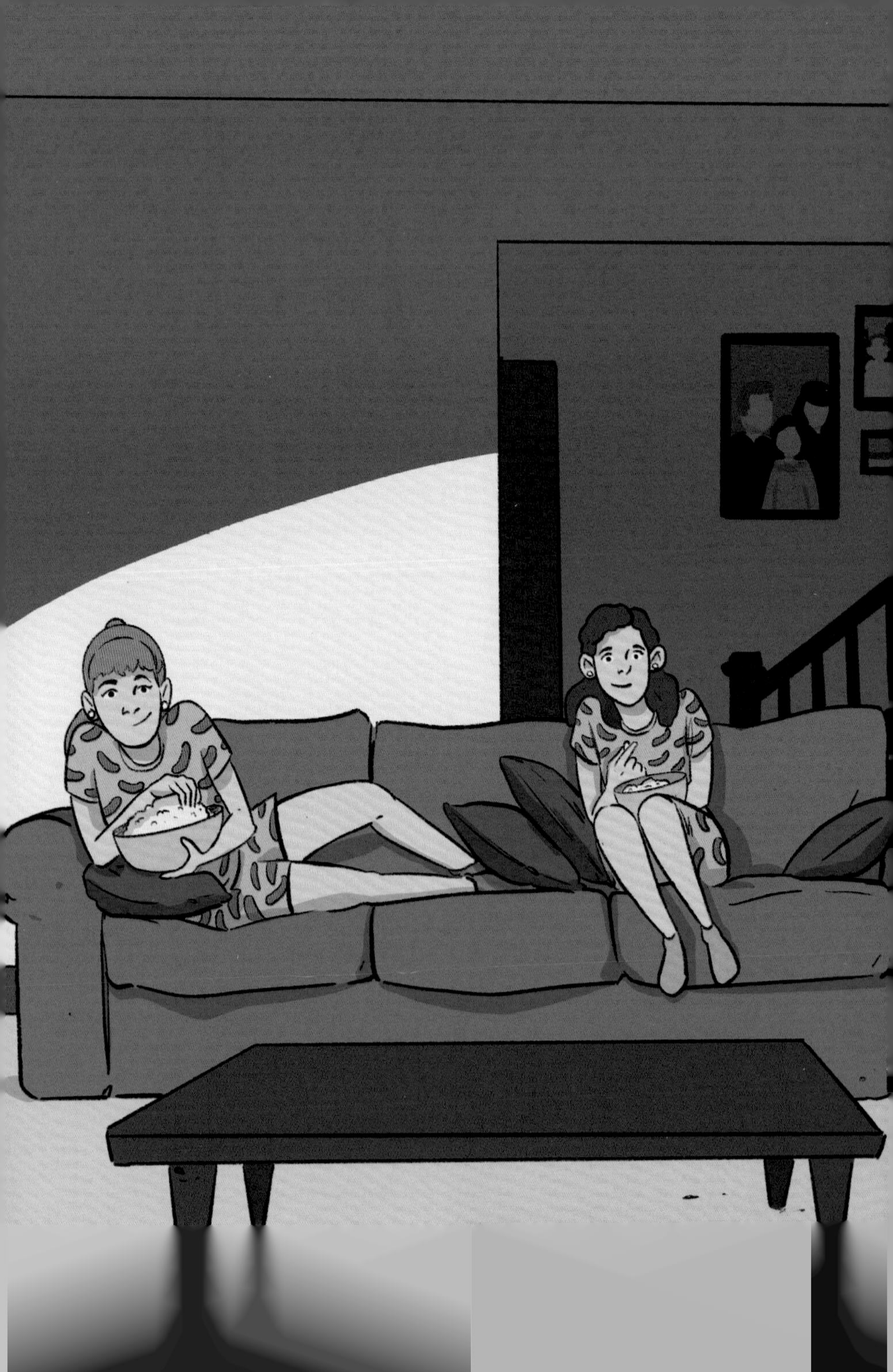

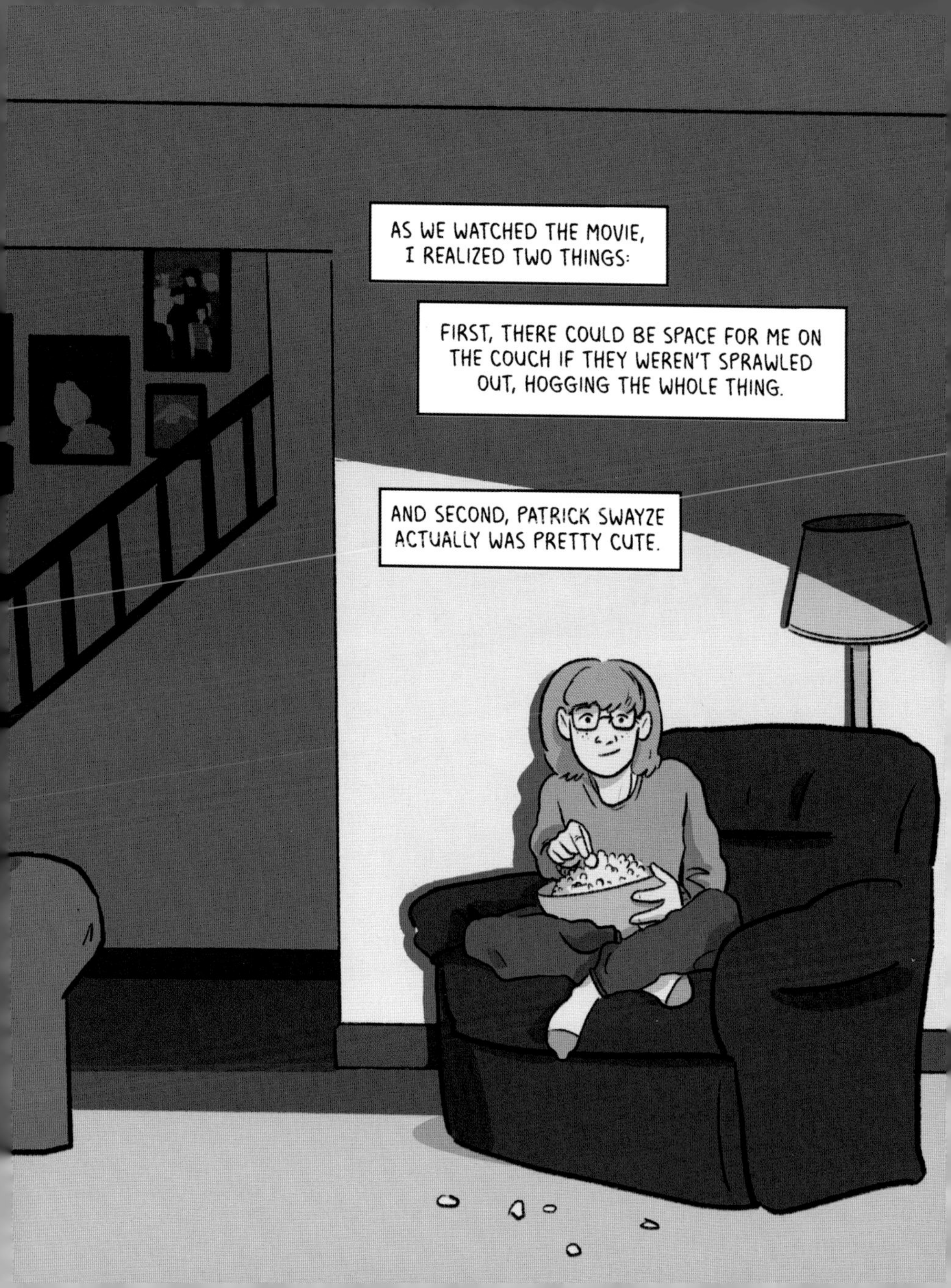
AS WE WATCHED THE MOVIE, I REALIZED TWO THINGS:
FIRST, THERE COULD BE SPACE FOR ME ON THE COUCH IF THEY WEREN'T SPRAWLED OUT, HOGGING THE WHOLE THING.
AND SECOND, PATRICK SWAYZE ACTUALLY WAS PRETTY CUTE.

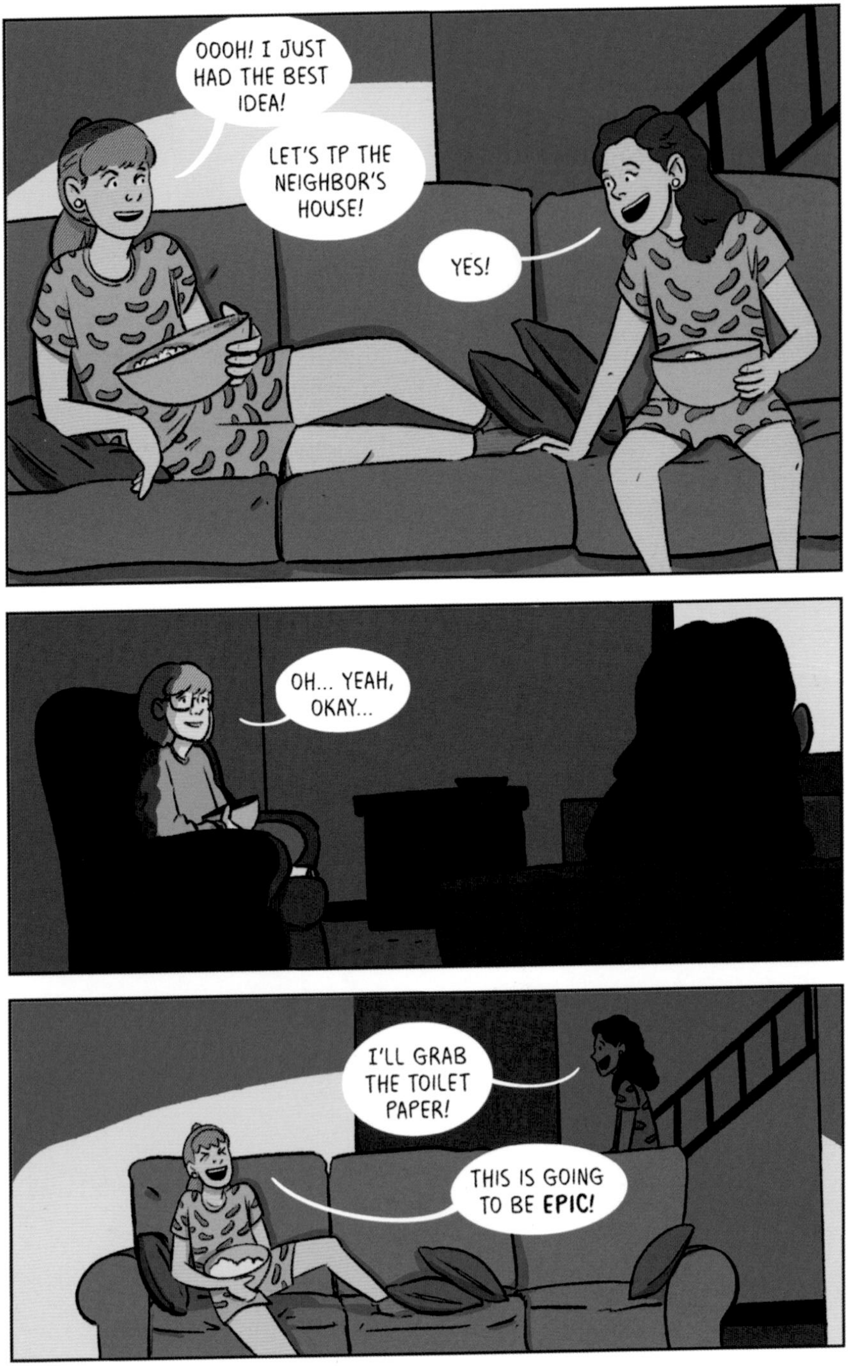
OOOH! I JUST HAD THE BEST IDEA!
LET'S TP THE NEIGHBOR'S HOUSE!
YES!
OH... YEAH, OKAY...
I'LL GRAB THE TOILET PAPER!
THIS IS GOING TO BE **EPIC!**

I COULDN'T BELIEVE BREE WAS SO EXCITED. DIDN'T SHE REALIZE HOW WRONG IT WAS TO TP SOMEONE'S HOUSE?

I WANTED TO TELL THEM THAT I'D JUST WAIT THERE UNTIL THEY GOT BACK, BUT I DIDN'T WANT AVA TO THINK I WAS A TOTAL LOSER.

COME ON!

THIS DOESN'T SEEM RIGHT... I MEAN, THE GUY WHO LIVES HERE IS LIKE A HUNDRED YEARS OLD, AND HE'LL HAVE TO CLEAN THIS UP TOMORROW...

STOP RUINING THE FUN OR JUST GO BACK TO THE HOUSE. JEEZ.

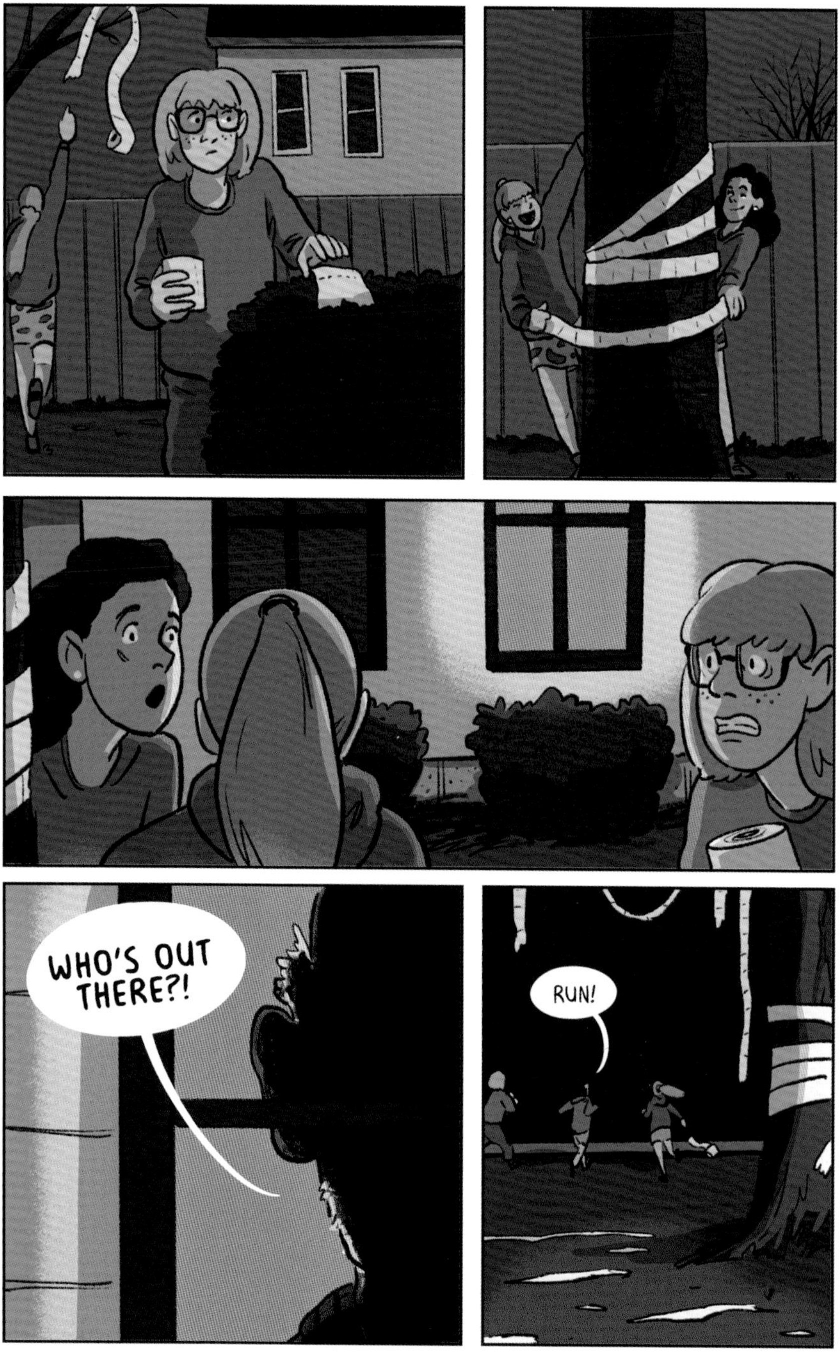
WHO'S OUT THERE?!
RUN!

I CAN'T BELIEVE WE WERE ALMOST CAUGHT!

I KNOW! I WAS **FREAKING OUT!**

I'M GONNA GRAB A SNACK...

I KEPT PICTURING THE OLD GUY LOOKING OUT HIS WINDOW AND SEEING HIS YARD. I FELT SO GUILTY.

AND NOW AVA THOUGHT I WAS A TOTAL PARTY POOPER.

COULD THIS NIGHT GET ANY WORSE?

WHIPP CREAM

SUDDENLY, I HAD AN IDEA—ONE THAT WOULD FIX THE NIGHT AND SHOW AVA THAT I DID KNOW HOW TO HAVE FUN.

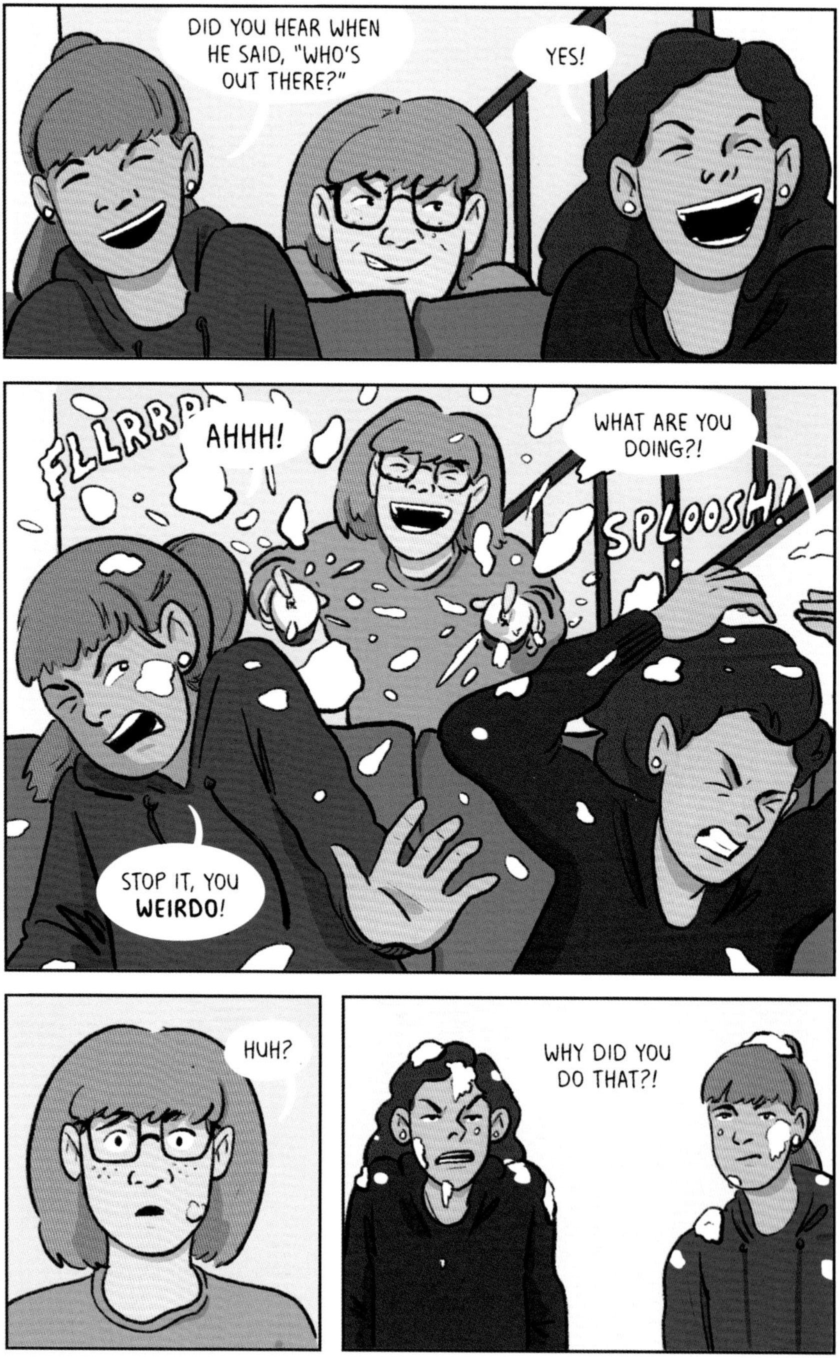
DID YOU HEAR WHEN HE SAID, "WHO'S OUT THERE?"
YES!
FLLRRR
AHHH!
WHAT ARE YOU DOING?!
SPLOOSH!
STOP IT, YOU **WEIRDO**!
HUH?
WHY DID YOU DO THAT?!

I'M SORRY. I THOUGHT IT WOULD BE FUNNY. WE USED TO HAVE FOOD FIGHTS ALL THE TIME...

WE **USED TO.** WE AREN'T LITTLE KIDS ANYMORE, MISTY.

UGH. AND MY DAD IS GOING TO BE SO MAD ABOUT THE MESS.

NOW I HAVE TO WASH MY HAIR.

I'LL STAY DOWN HERE AND CLEAN UP...

WHAT IN THE WORLD JUST HAPPENED? HAD MY BEST FRIEND COMPLETELY VANISHED?

LET'S PLAY A GAME.

OKAY. WHAT KIND OF GAME?

WELL, IT'S SORT OF LIKE TRUTH OR DARE BUT WITHOUT THE DARES.

SO, A GAME OF TRUTH?

KIND OF.

EXCEPT WE'LL GO AROUND AND TELL THE TRUTH ABOUT WHAT WE THOUGHT OF EACH OTHER WHEN WE FIRST MET VERSUS WHAT WE THINK NOW. IT'LL BE FUNNY TO COMPARE.

I REALLY DIDN'T UNDERSTAND THIS "GAME," BUT CONSIDERING I'D ALREADY RUINED THEIR NIGHT, PLAYING WAS THE LEAST I COULD DO.

OKAY, SURE.

ALL RIGHT, I'LL GO FIRST.

AVA, WHEN I FIRST MET YOU, I THOUGHT YOU WERE SUPER PRETTY AND REALLY COOL. AND I STILL DO!

AWW! THAT'S SO NICE! THANK YOU!

OKAY, I'LL GO NOW.

SO, MISTY, WHEN I FIRST MET YOU, I THOUGHT YOU WERE SO WEIRD. YOU WERE **LOUD** AND **OBNOXIOUS** AND SO **COMPETITIVE**.

AND BREE WAS BASICALLY YOUR ONLY FRIEND BESIDES A BUNCH OF BOYS.

OH, AND YOUR BAGGY CLOTHES—I COULDN'T FIGURE OUT WHY YOU DRESSED LIKE THAT.

NOW, MOST OF THOSE THINGS ARE STILL TRUE... AND YOU CHOOSE TO KEEP YOUR HAIR LOOKING LIKE THAT.

PLUS, YOU PLAY FOOTBALL. I DON'T KNOW. I JUST DON'T GET YOU.

YEAH, PLAYING FOOTBALL IS WEIRD. I STILL DON'T UNDERSTAND WHY YOU KEPT PLAYING.

MISTY? ARE YOU OKAY?

YEAH, I'M JUST TIRED. I FEEL LIKE I COULD SLEEP THOUGH AN EARTHQUAKE RIGHT NOW.

I'M GONNA GO TO SLEEP, BUT YOU CAN KEEP PLAYING THE GAME. IT WON'T BOTHER ME.

THAT WAS WHEN I REALIZED AVA AND I WOULD **NEVER** BE FRIENDS—AND I DIDN'T WANNA BE. WE WERE NOTHING ALIKE.

BUT THE WORST PART WAS THAT BREE AND I HAD GROWN APART, AND I WAS PRETTY SURE WE WEREN'T FRIENDS ANYMORE, EITHER.

SO, DID YOU HAVE FUN?

YEAH.

WELL, THAT'S GOOD.

OH NO. LOOK AT THAT.

THAT POOR OLD MAN HAS TO CLEAN UP HIS YARD. IT REALLY IS A SHAME SOMEONE WOULD DO THAT TO HIM...

YEAH, THAT'S REALLY MESSED UP.

I WAS SURE MY MOM KNEW WE DID IT, BUT I DIDN'T WANT TO ADMIT IT TO HER. I WAS TOO ASHAMED.

WE DIDN'T TALK THE REST OF THE WAY HOME.

I'M GONNA GO TO MY ROOM.

I WAS IN THE WORST MOOD, AND I REALLY JUST WANTED TO BE ALONE.

HEY, MISTY! DO YOU WANNA PLAY A BOARD GAME? OR DRAW WITH ME?

UGH! STOP ASKING ME TO PLAY ALL THE TIME! I DON'T WANNA PLAY WITH YOU!

SLAM

FINE! SORRY! I'LL NEVER ASK AGAIN!

I COULDN'T WAIT FOR MY GAME LATER. AT FOOTBALL, I DIDN'T HAVE TO WORRY ABOUT WHETHER I WAS COOL OR WEIRD OR PRETTY. I COULD JUST FOCUS ON THE GAME.

AND HOPEFULLY TONIGHT I'D GET TO SHOW MY TEAM THAT I COULD BE MORE THAN AN OFFENSIVE TACKLE.

CHAPTER 8

THAT EVENING, THE STANDS WERE PACKED. EVEN MOM CAME TO THE GAME. BUT THE SCORE WAS CLOSE, SO I KNEW THERE WAS NO WAY COACH G WAS GONNA GIVE ME A SHOT AT A NEW POSITION.

BUT THEN...

MISTY! GET IN THERE!

OH, AND MISTY, DO **NOT** LET THEM GET THROUGH!

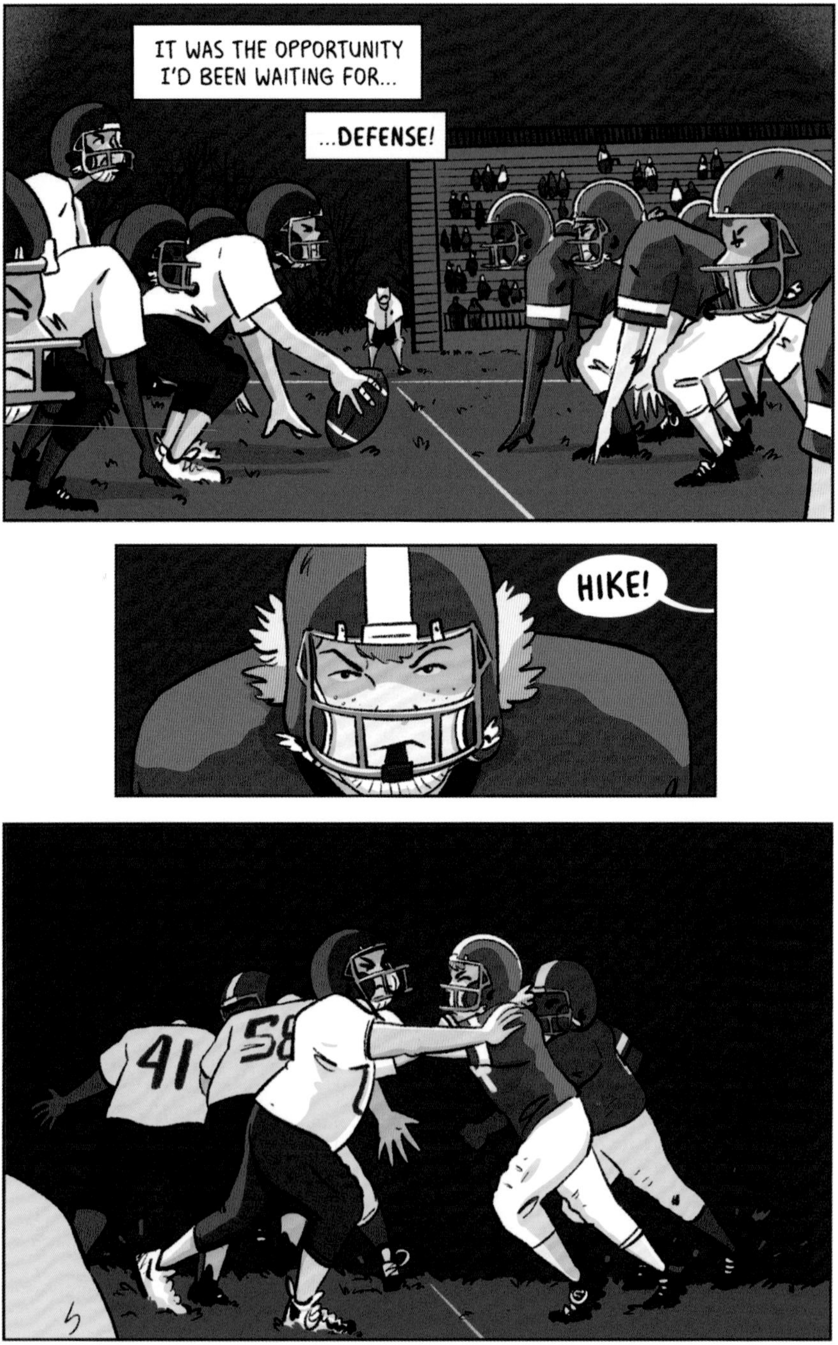
IT WAS THE OPPORTUNITY I'D BEEN WAITING FOR...
...DEFENSE!
HIKE!
41
58

THEIR OFFENSE WAS GOOD.

BUT I WASN'T GONNA LET THE RUNNING BACK GET PAST ME.

BOOM!

NO GAIN!

SHE STOPPED THEM!

GO, MISTY!

ALL RIGHT, MISTY!

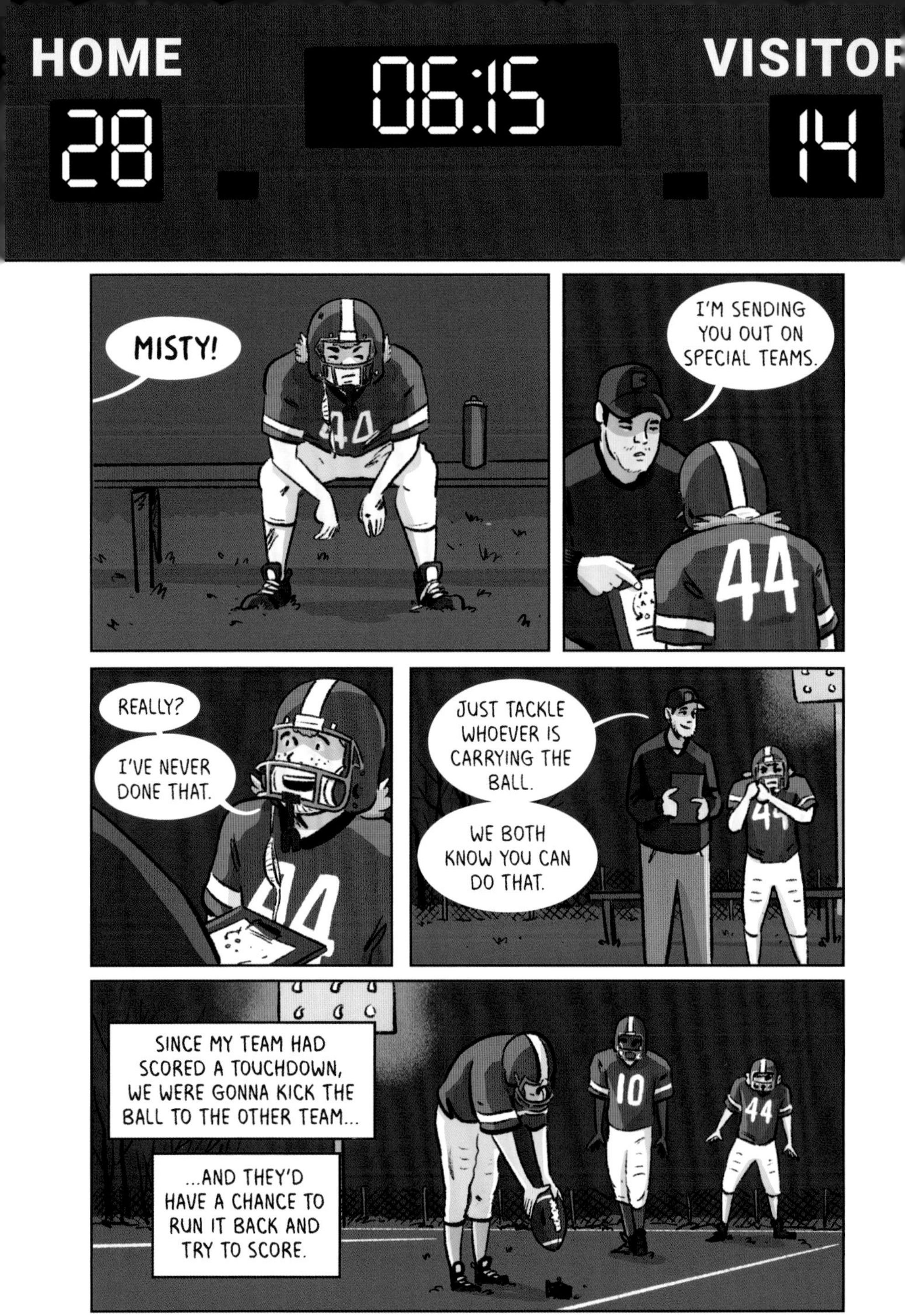
HOME
06:15
VISITOR
28
14
MISTY!
I'M SENDING YOU OUT ON SPECIAL TEAMS.
REALLY?
I'VE NEVER DONE THAT.
JUST TACKLE WHOEVER IS CARRYING THE BALL.
WE BOTH KNOW YOU CAN DO THAT.
SINCE MY TEAM HAD SCORED A TOUCHDOWN, WE WERE GONNA KICK THE BALL TO THE OTHER TEAM...
...AND THEY'D HAVE A CHANCE TO RUN IT BACK AND TRY TO SCORE.

MY JOB WAS TO STOP THEM.

AND I WAS READY.

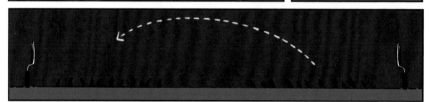

GET HIM!

THIS KID WAS REALLY FAST.

BUT I KNEW I COULD CATCH HIM.

I JUST HAD TO GET PAST THIS BLOCK.

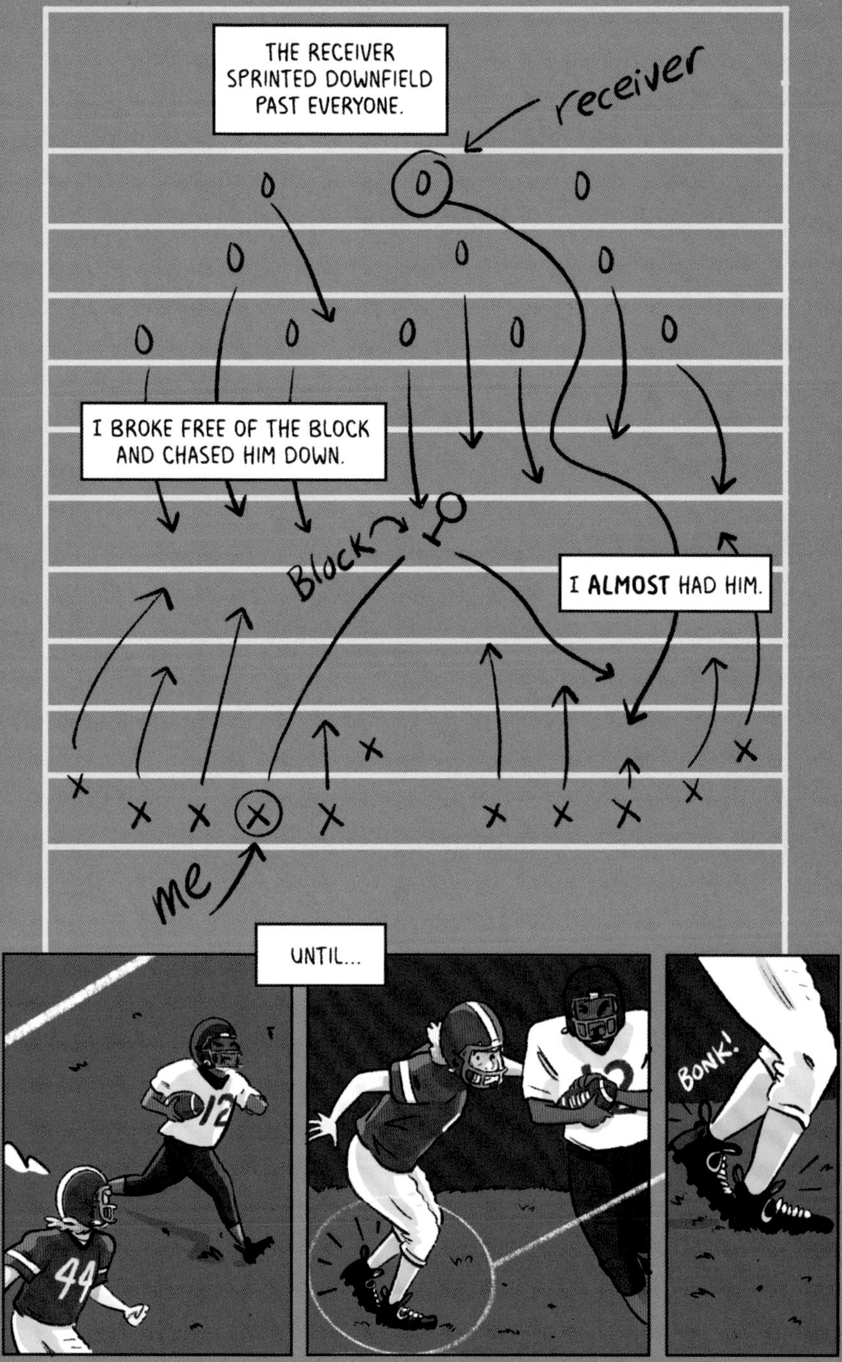
THE RECEIVER SPRINTED DOWNFIELD PAST EVERYONE.
receiver
I BROKE FREE OF THE BLOCK AND CHASED HIM DOWN.
Block
I ALMOST HAD HIM.
me
UNTIL...
BONK!

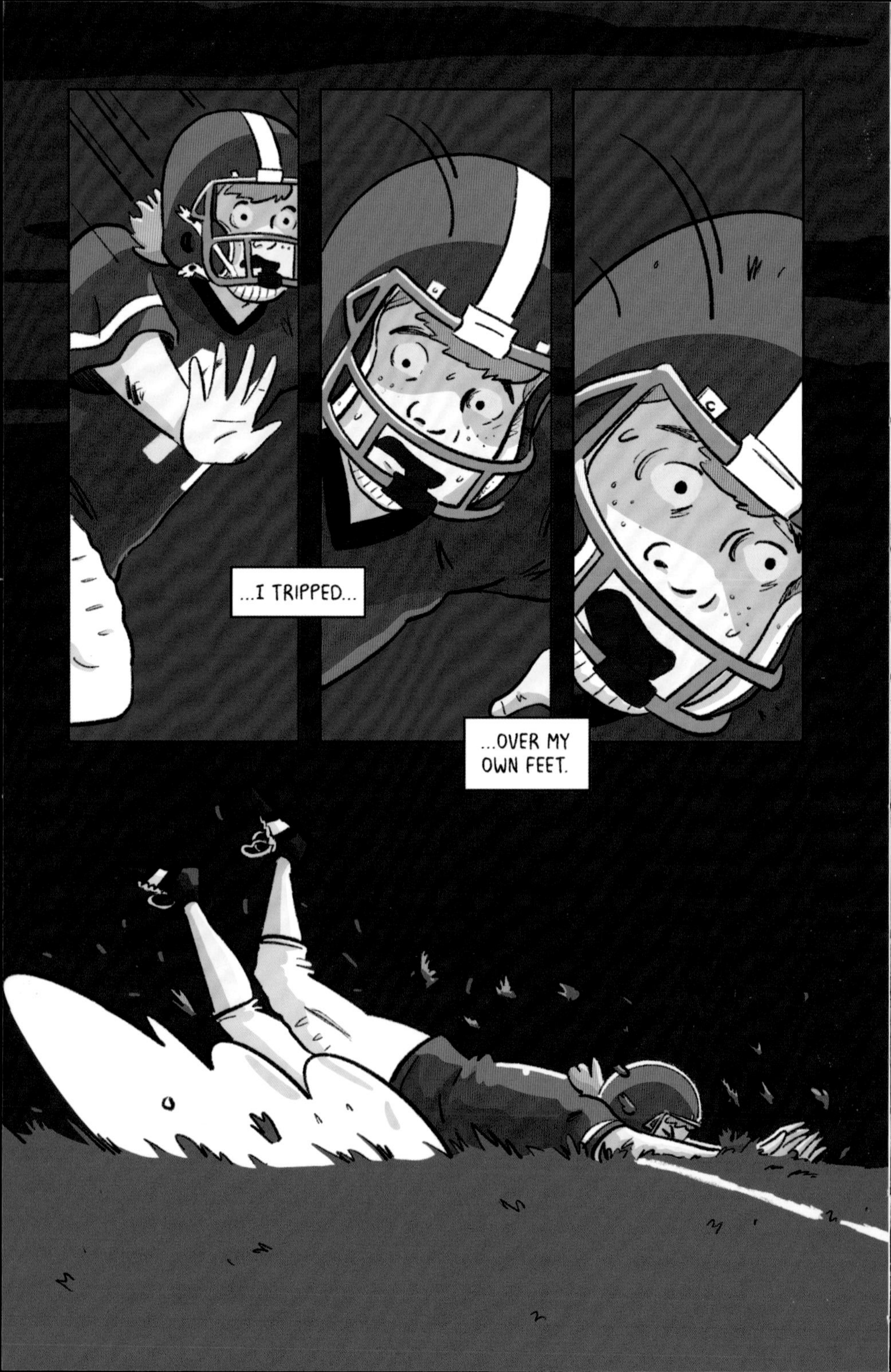
...I TRIPPED...
...OVER MY OWN FEET.

TOUCHDOWN!

NO...

EVERYONE OFF THE FIELD!

SO MANY PEOPLE SAW ME GET A FACEFUL OF DIRT.

I JUST WANTED TO HIDE.

LATER.

HOME

02:03

28

VISITOR

21

IT WAS MY CHANCE AT HALFBACK—MY CHANCE TO SCORE A TOUCHDOWN.

I JUST HAD TO SHAKE OFF THE EMBARRASSMENT FROM EARLIER AND MAKE IT TO THE END ZONE.

HIKE!

I RECEIVED THE HANDOFF WITHOUT FUMBLING—JUST LIKE I'D PRACTICED A THOUSAND TIMES.

THE OFFENSIVE LINE CREATED A HOLE FOR ME. IT WAS **PERFECT**.

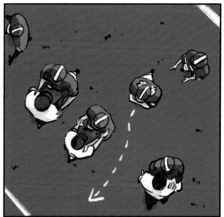

AND I MADE IT THROUGH UNTOUCHED!

OR SO I THOUGHT...

WHERE DID HE COME FROM?

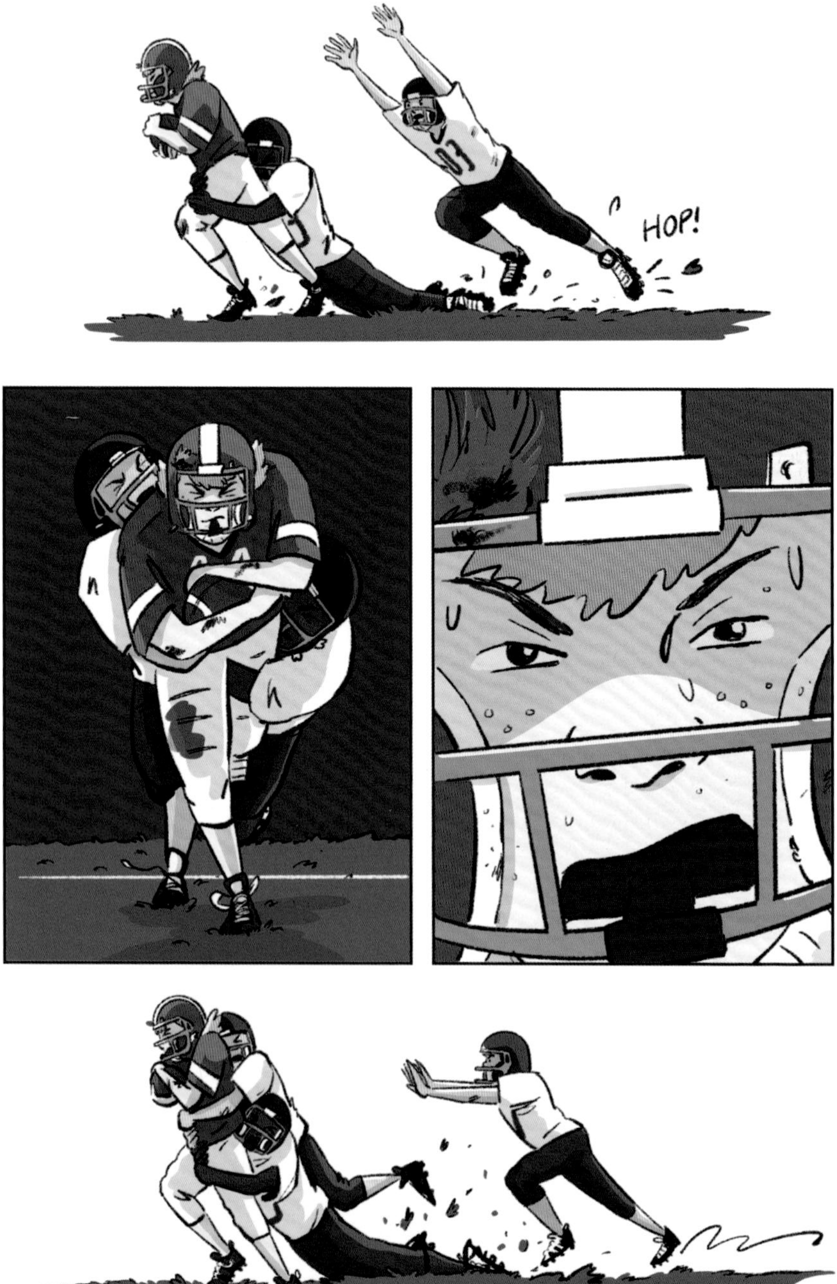
HOP!

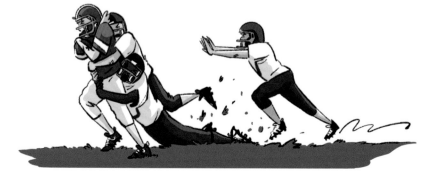

BOOM!

KEEP PUSHING!

GO!

GO, MISTY!

YEEEEEESSSSSS!

THE BOYS DIDN'T TAKE ME DOWN, BUT SINCE I WASN'T ACTUALLY MOVING FORWARD ANYMORE, THE REFEREE ENDED THE PLAY.

BRING IT IN, MISTY!

WHAT?

IS HE SERIOUS RIGHT NOW?! THAT WAS MY ONLY CHANCE?

I KNEW I COULD DO BETTER THAN THAT! I HATED THAT I WAS BEING PULLED OUT.

HOME
28

LATER.

AND THAT'S THE END OF THE GAME, FOLKS!

THE BEARS WIN AGAIN!

HOME 28 0 00:00

DOWN TO GO ON

GREAT JOB TONIGHT, MISTY.

ESPECIALLY FOR BEING YOUR FIRST TIME PLAYING THOSE NEW POSITIONS!

BUT YOU'RE GOING TO HAVE TO WORK ON THAT SPORTSMANSHIP.

YEAH... SORRY, COACH.

CHEER UP. WE WON!

PLAYOFFS, HERE WE COME! HAVE A GOOD NIGHT!

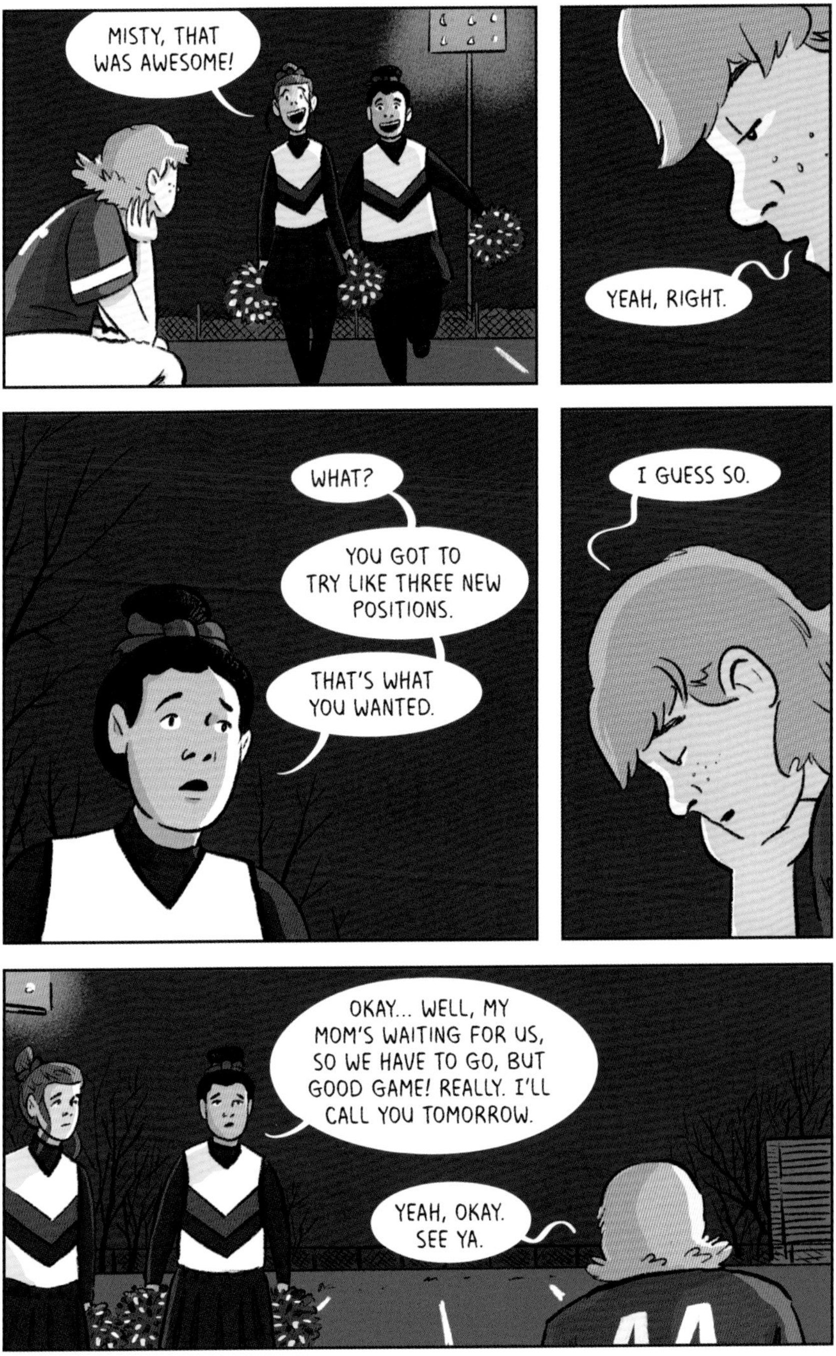
MISTY, THAT WAS AWESOME!
YEAH, RIGHT.
WHAT?
YOU GOT TO TRY LIKE THREE NEW POSITIONS.
THAT'S WHAT YOU WANTED.
I GUESS SO.
OKAY... WELL, MY MOM'S WAITING FOR US, SO WE HAVE TO GO, BUT GOOD GAME! REALLY. I'LL CALL YOU TOMORROW.
YEAH, OKAY. SEE YA.

MISTY! THAT WAS SO MUCH FUN TO WATCH!

YOU WERE FANTASTIC!

VERY RAD.

YEAH... GREAT...

DO YOU WANT TO GO GET A BITE TO EAT OR SOMETHING?

TO CELEBRATE?

THANKS...

BUT CAN WE JUST GO HOME?

BETWEEN THE SLEEPOVER AND THE GAME, I WAS IN AN AWFUL MOOD. I REALLY DIDN'T FEEL LIKE CELEBRATING ANYTHING.

LATER THAT NIGHT.

HEY, HONEY.

I JUST WANTED TO CHECK ON YOU.

I'M FINE.

ARE YOU SURE?

YOU'VE SEEMED UPSET EVER SINCE YOU GOT HOME THIS MORNING.

DO YOU WANT TO TALK ABOUT IT?

OH, SO NOW YOU SUDDENLY HAVE TIME FOR ME?

WHAT?

I'M JUST SURPRISED IS ALL.

USUALLY, YOU'RE TOO **BUSY** OR TOO **TIRED**.

I DON'T APPRECIATE YOUR ATTITUDE, YOUNG LADY.

I'M SORRY, BUT THE TWINS ARE STILL BASICALLY BABIES. THEY REQUIRE A LOT OF TIME AND ATTENTION RIGHT NOW.

OBVIOUSLY!

STOP IT.

I RARELY ASK ANY OF YOU TO HELP WITH ANYTHING AROUND THE HOUSE, AND IT'S EXHAUSTING. I'M DOING THE BEST I CAN.

UGH. WHATEVER! CAN YOU PLEASE GO NOW? I DON'T WANNA TALK.

MOM DIDN'T SAY ANYTHING ELSE. SHE JUST LEFT, LOOKING SAD.

OF COURSE, SHE WAS RIGHT—NONE OF US HELPED HER. LIKE, EVER.

YELLING AT HER DIDN'T MAKE ME FEEL BETTER. NOW I WAS ANGRY **AND** I FELT BAD, WHICH ONLY MADE ME ANGRIER.

I WISHED I COULD STAY IN MY ROOM FOREVER.

CHAPTER 9

NEXT FRIDAY NIGHT.

AFTER A WEEK OF HARDLY TALKING TO MOM AND AVOIDING BREE AND AVA AS MUCH AS POSSIBLE, I WAS EXCITED TO LET LOOSE AND DANCE.

A SLOW SONG!

ARE YOU GONNA ASK BEN TO DANCE?

OH, I DON'T KNOW. I...

COME ON! YOU CAN DO IT.

BE AGGRESSIVE! BE-E AGGRESSIVE!

OKAY. YEAH, ALL RIGHT. I'M GOING TO GO FOR IT.

AMANDA WAS SO QUIET AND SHY...

...AND SEEING HER BE BRAVE ENOUGH TO ASK BEN TO DANCE WAS GIVING ME COURAGE.

AW, SHE'S ALL GROWN-UP.

WE'RE IN SEVENTH GRADE.

EH, DETAILS.

YEP. I WAS GONNA DO IT. I WAS GONNA ASK CHARLIE TO DANCE WITH ME.

EXCEPT THE SICK FEELING WAS BACK, AND MY FEET REFUSED TO MOVE.

YEAH, NO WAY. NOT HAPPENING.

MAYBE HE'S GONNA ASK ME TO DANCE...

HE'S COMING OVER HERE. OH MY GOSH. OH MY GOSH. OH MY GOSH.

WHAT THE...?

WAS IT JUST ME OR WAS THIS THE WORST DANCE EVER?

SO, SHALL WE?

SURE.

I REFUSED TO LET A BOY RUIN MY NIGHT.

I WAS ABLE TO FORGET ABOUT CHARLIE...

...(WELL, MOSTLY)...

I LOVE THIS SONG!

...AND I WAS HAVING A **BLAST**!

UNTIL...

HEY, MISTY!

HI...

THOSE ARE SOME **INTERESTING** DANCE MOVES...

...BUT MAYBE YOU SHOULD SAVE THEM FOR WHEN YOU'RE NOT IN PUBLIC.

I WANTED TO IGNORE HER. I WANTED TO LAUGH IT OFF LIKE IT DIDN'T MATTER WHAT SHE SAID. BUT I COULDN'T TAKE IT ANYMORE.

UGH! JUST SHUT UP ALREADY, BREE!

I— WHAT? I WAS JUST KIDDING.

WELL, IT ISN'T FUNNY!

ALL YOU DO IS MAKE FUN OF ME! YOU ONLY EVER HAVE MEAN THINGS TO SAY, AND I'M SICK OF IT!

DRAMA QUEEN...

YOU CAN SHUT UP, TOO. JUST LEAVE ME ALONE. BOTH OF YOU.

BAM!

MISTY?

MISTY, ARE YOU IN THERE?

NO.

ARE YOU OKAY?

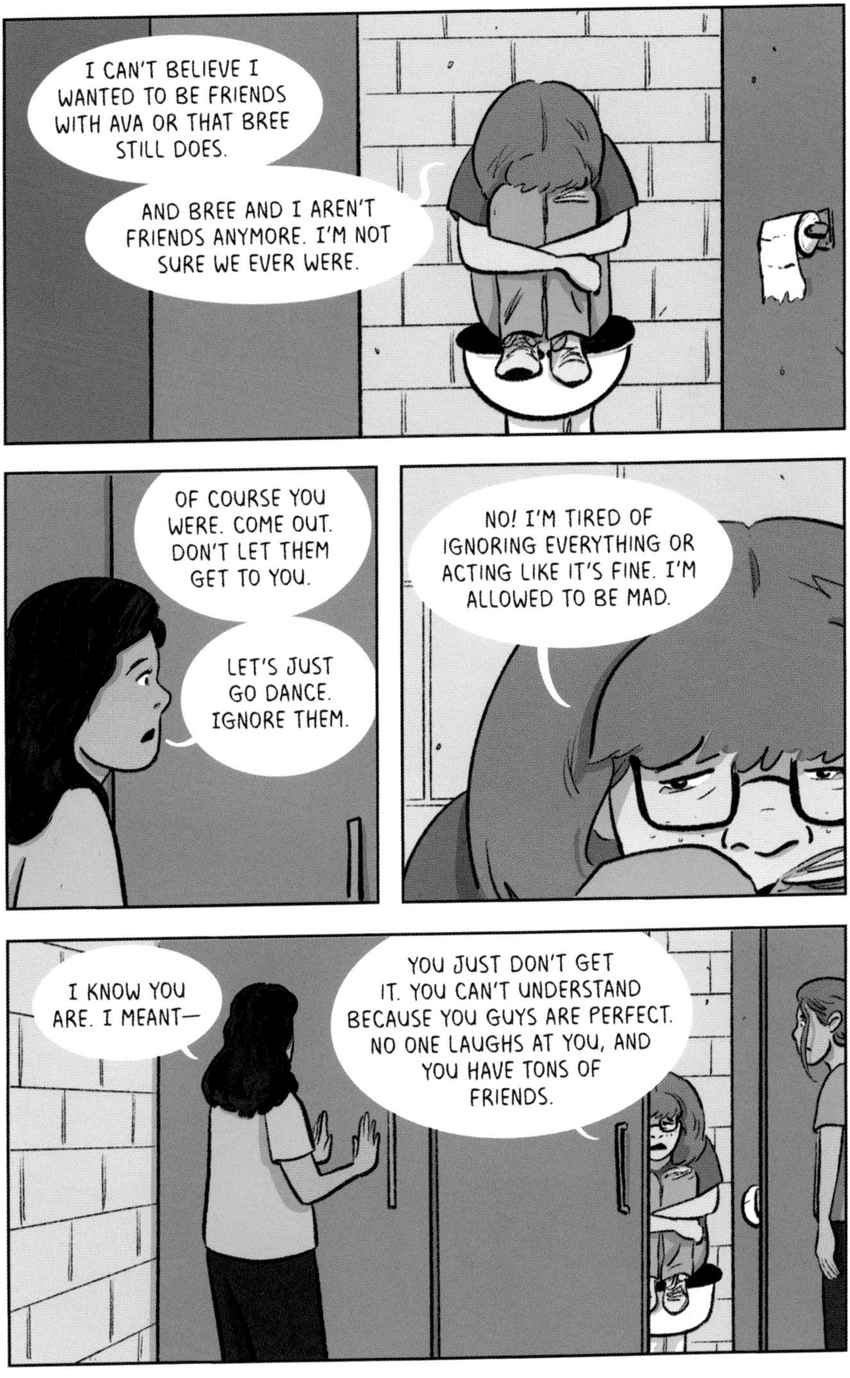
I CAN'T BELIEVE I WANTED TO BE FRIENDS WITH AVA OR THAT BREE STILL DOES.
AND BREE AND I AREN'T FRIENDS ANYMORE. I'M NOT SURE WE EVER WERE.
OF COURSE YOU WERE. COME OUT. DON'T LET THEM GET TO YOU.
LET'S JUST GO DANCE. IGNORE THEM.
NO! I'M TIRED OF IGNORING EVERYTHING OR ACTING LIKE IT'S FINE. I'M ALLOWED TO BE MAD.
I KNOW YOU ARE. I MEANT—
YOU JUST DON'T GET IT. YOU CAN'T UNDERSTAND BECAUSE YOU GUYS ARE PERFECT. NO ONE LAUGHS AT YOU, AND YOU HAVE TONS OF FRIENDS.

WE AREN'T PERFECT, AND YOU HAVE FRIENDS, TOO. THE FOOTBALL GUYS—

YEAH, RIGHT!

THEY'RE HARDLY FRIENDS. IN FACT, MOST OF THE TIME, I DON'T FEEL LIKE I HAVE **ANY** FRIENDS.

OUCH.

I THOUGHT **WE** WERE YOUR FRIENDS.

YOU ARE MY FRIENDS. I DIDN'T—

NO. WE HEARD YOU LOUD AND CLEAR.

WE'RE JUST THE GIRLS YOU HANG OUT WITH WHEN AVA AND BREE DON'T WANT TO HANG OUT WITH YOU.

WHAT?

NO.

I'M GOING TO GO BACK OUT THERE. GOOD LUCK FIXING THINGS WITH YOUR REAL FRIENDS, MISTY.

YEAH, I'M COMING WITH YOU.

I COULDN'T BELIEVE I'D SAID THAT TO THEM. I DIDN'T EVEN MEAN IT.

MY LIFE WAS A TOTAL DISASTER. THIS WAS **NOT** HOW SEVENTH GRADE WAS SUPPOSED TO GO.

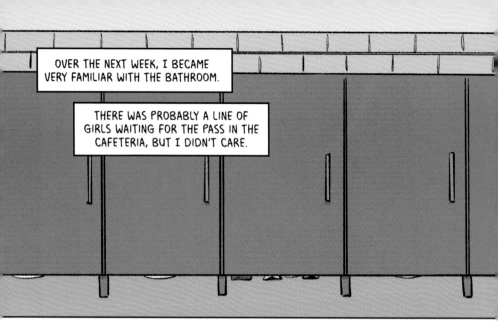

OVER THE NEXT WEEK, I BECAME VERY FAMILIAR WITH THE BATHROOM.

THERE WAS PROBABLY A LINE OF GIRLS WAITING FOR THE PASS IN THE CAFETERIA, BUT I DIDN'T CARE.

I SPENT LUNCH AVOIDING PRETTY MUCH EVERYONE.

I HARDLY ATE. THE BATHROOM SMELLED BAD, AND IT FELT TOO GROSS TO EAT ON A TOILET.

I WASN'T VERY HUNGRY, ANYWAY.

OF ALL THE THINGS THAT WERE WRONG RIGHT NOW, I WAS MOST UPSET ABOUT JENNA AND AMANDA BEING MAD AT ME.

BUT THERE WAS NO WAY THEY WOULD EVER FORGIVE ME.

EVERYTHING WAS IN SHAMBLES, BUT I WAS GOING TO HAVE TO FORGET ALL THAT IF MY TEAM WAS GOING TO GO TO THE CHAMPIONSHIP.

IS THAT... A GIRL?

THAT'S DEFINITELY A GIRL. SO COOL.

I COULDN'T WAIT TO TELL BREE THAT ANOTHER GIRL WAS PLAYING FOOTBALL!

...IF WE EVER TALKED AGAIN.

EITHER WAY, THIS GIRL WAS MY COMPETITION, AND I WAS HERE TO WIN. I NEEDED TO GO JUST AS HARD AS I ALWAYS DID.

HIKE!

WOMP!

OH MY GOSH. DID I JUST BREAK ONE OF HER BONES?

I SWEAR I HEARD HER BODY CRACK.

ARE YOU OKAY?

YEAH, I'M FINE. NO WORRIES.

I HADN'T EXPECTED HER TO GO DOWN SO EASILY.

I'M SO SORRY.

DON'T BE!

I KNEW THIS GIRL HAD TO BE TOUGH IN ORDER TO TAKE HITS ALL THE TIME, BUT STILL, I WAS SORT OF AFRAID I WAS GONNA SERIOUSLY INJURE HER.

SO I WENT EASY ON HER...

...WHICH LED TO THE LONGEST, MOST BORING GAME EVER FOR ME.

MOM MADE IT TO MY GAME, AND I WOULD HAVE BEEN EXCITED IF I WASN'T STILL FEELING REALLY BAD ABOUT OUR FIGHT.

WE WON!

GOOD GAME.

THANKS...

I'M NOT EXACTLY THE BEST PLAYER, BUT I LOVE FOOTBALL.

IT'S AWESOME SEEING ANOTHER GIRL ON THE FIELD.

YEAH, MY TEAMMATES AND MY COACH TAKE IT EASY ON ME BECAUSE I'M A GIRL. THEY'RE SUPER PROTECTIVE OF ME, WHICH IS PROBABLY WHY I WAS PITTED AGAINST YOU.

A LOT OF GOOD THAT DID.

I DIDN'T TELL HER, BUT SHE WAS LUCKY SHE WAS PITTED AGAINST ME. THE BOYS ON MY TEAM DID **NOT** GO EASY ON GIRLS.

SUDDENLY, I REALIZED HOW LUCKY I WAS.

MY TEAMMATES PUSHED ME TO BE A BETTER PLAYER AND ATHLETE EVERY SINGLE DAY BY NEVER TAKING IT EASY ON ME.

MAYBE WE CAN HANG OUT SOMETIME?

AND PRACTICE?

FOR SURE!

THIS GIRL MADE ME FEEL LIKE MAYBE IT WASN'T ALL THAT WEIRD THAT I PLAYED FOOTBALL. LIKE MAYBE BREE AND AVA WERE WRONG.

HOW COME THEY GOT TO DECIDE WHAT WAS COOL, ANYWAY?

I WASN'T SURE WHY I EVER CARED ABOUT BEING FRIENDS WITH AVA OR BEING POPULAR. WHEN I WAS WITH JENNA AND AMANDA, I COULD JUST BE... ME, AND THAT'S ALL I WANTED.

I HAD MESSED UP A LOT THE LAST FEW WEEKS, AND NOW I NEEDED TO FIX THINGS.

CHAPTER 10

I'D BEEN GOING BONKERS AVOIDING MOM. I REALLY MISSED HER, AND I OWED HER AN APOLOGY.

HEY, MOM... CAN WE TALK?

SURE. WHAT'S UP?

I GUESS I JUST WANTED TO SAY THAT I SHOULDN'T HAVE SAID THOSE THINGS TO YOU.

YOU WERE RIGHT.

YOU DON'T ASK US TO DO ANYTHING TO HELP YOU—AND WE DON'T EXACTLY VOLUNTEER. I'M REALLY SORRY. I KNOW IT'S HARD HAVING THE TWINS.

AND I'M SORRY THAT IT'S HARD FOR ME TO MAKE TIME FOR EVERYTHING. YOU KNOW I LOVE YOU, THOUGH, RIGHT?

YEAH, I KNOW.

AND I PROMISE THINGS WILL GET EASIER AS THE TWINS GET OLDER.

I KNOW THAT, TOO.

WELL, OKAY, THEN, MRS. KNOW-IT-ALL.

WAAAAA

OH! I GOT 'EM! YOU JUST **RELAX**!

I'M FOLDING THE LAUNDRY...

RIGHT. OR THAT. BUT I HAVE THE TWINS!

THANKS. OH, AND MISTY, CAN YOU DO ME ANOTHER FAVOR?

SURE.

TAKE IT A LITTLE EASIER ON YOUR SISTER? SHE'S PROBABLY FEELING THE EXACT SAME WAY YOU ARE.

YEAH, I CAN DO THAT.

I'D NEVER THOUGHT ABOUT THAT, BUT MOM WAS PROBABLY RIGHT.

ONCE I GOT THE TWINS TO CALM DOWN, I DECIDED THERE WAS NO TIME LIKE THE PRESENT TO MAKE THINGS RIGHT WITH LIV... EVEN IF I DIDN'T LIKE WHAT I WAS ABOUT TO DO...

HEY, LIV, CAN I PLAY?

REALLY?

YEAH, DOES THE MERMAID BARBIE OFFER STILL STAND?

EEEK! YEAH!

OKAY, SO, I WASN'T INTO BARBIES. BUT LIV'S EXCITEMENT WAS WORTH IT. NOW I JUST HAD TO TALK TO JENNA AND AMANDA.

AT LUNCH ON MONDAY, I FINALLY WENT TO THE CAFETERIA.

BUT MY NERVES WERE MAKING ME FEEL SICK AGAIN, SO MAYBE I SHOULD HAVE GONE TO THE BATHROOM INSTEAD...

HEY, GUYS.

CAN I SIT WITH YOU?

UM, I DON'T KNOW WHY YOU WOULDN'T WANT TO SIT WITH **FRIENDS** INSTEAD, BUT SURE.

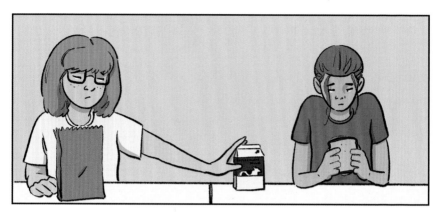

I OWED YOU A CHOCOLATE MILK FROM WHEN YOU HELPED ME ON THE FIRST DAY OF SCHOOL, AND I FORGOT...

I GUESS I'VE BEEN KIND OF DISTRACTED.

SIGH.

I'M SO, SO, SO SORRY. I'M THE WORST.

YOU GUYS **ARE** MY FRIENDS. ACTUALLY, THIS YEAR YOU'VE KIND OF BEEN MY BEST FRIENDS. I WAS UPSET ABOUT BREE, AND I SHOULDN'T HAVE SAID WHAT I SAID!

I FEEL HORRIBLE.

YOU'RE BACK TO WEARING YOUR OLD CLOTHES...

YEAH, THEY'RE WAY MORE ME.

AND I'M SO TIRED OF WORRYING ABOUT WHAT AVA THINKS. I DON'T THINK I CARE ANYMORE.

BUT I DO ACTUALLY LIKE MY HAIR, SO I'M GONNA KEEP IT BLOND.

GOOD.

THAT'S AWESOME.

YEAH...

SO, UH, DO YOU FORGIVE ME OR...

OF COURSE!

WE'VE MISSED YOU!

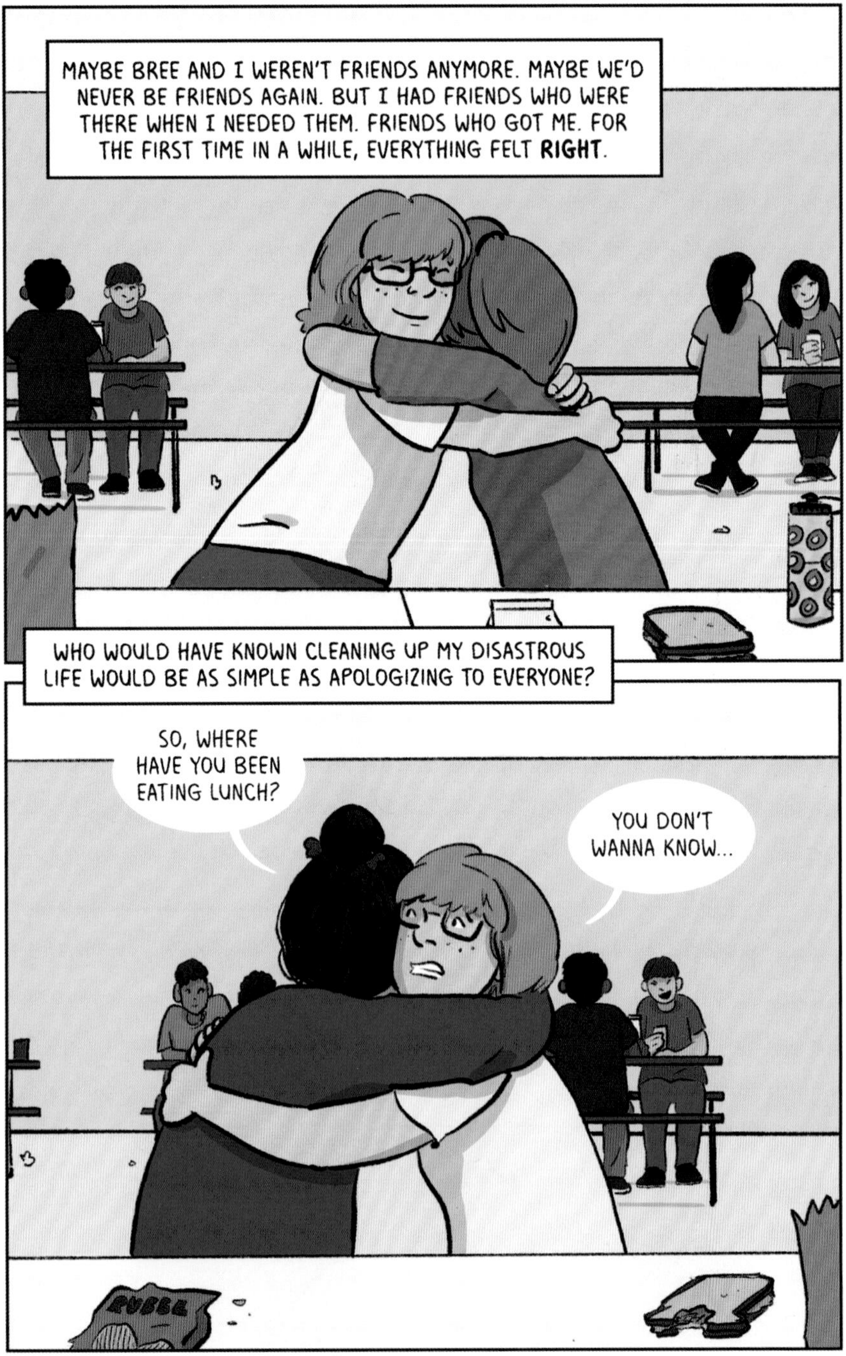
MAYBE BREE AND I WEREN'T FRIENDS ANYMORE. MAYBE WE'D NEVER BE FRIENDS AGAIN. BUT I HAD FRIENDS WHO WERE THERE WHEN I NEEDED THEM. FRIENDS WHO GOT ME. FOR THE FIRST TIME IN A WHILE, EVERYTHING FELT **RIGHT**.
WHO WOULD HAVE KNOWN CLEANING UP MY DISASTROUS LIFE WOULD BE AS SIMPLE AS APOLOGIZING TO EVERYONE?
SO, WHERE HAVE YOU BEEN EATING LUNCH?
YOU DON'T WANNA KNOW...

THE NEXT WEEKEND, JENNA, AMANDA, AND I GOT READY FOR THE BIG GAME.

OKAY, I THINK WE HAVE ENOUGH SIGNS FOR OUR FAMILIES AND ALL THE CHEERLEADERS.

YES, BUT IS THERE ENOUGH GLITTER ON THEM?

OH MY GOSH, NO MORE GLITTER, I'M BEGGING YOU! I'M ALREADY GONNA BE WEARING IT FOR WEEKS!

HA!

HOW ABOUT ICE CREAM INSTEAD?

YOU TWO FINISH UP WHILE I GET US SOME!

HOLY COW.

DIG IN!

OH BOY...

A LITTLE WHILE LATER.

I THINK I'M GOING TO THROW UP.

ICE CREAM AND BEST FRIENDS. LIFE DIDN'T GET ANY BETTER THAN THIS.

SAME.

LATER.

HI.

UM, HI. WHAT ARE YOU DOING HERE?

I WAS JUST RIDING AROUND AND WANTED TO COME OVER TO HANG OUT... LIKE WE USED TO... EXCEPT I REALIZED I COULDN'T... 'CAUSE YOU'RE MAD AT ME...

SO I WANTED TO SAY SORRY...

I REALLY WANT TO BE FRIENDS AGAIN.

OH...

AND?

I WAS WAITING FOR HER TO SAY WHAT SHE WAS SORRY FOR. MAYBE ADMIT THAT SHE'D BEEN MEAN OR **SOMETHING**.

AND I'M GOING TO COME TO YOUR FOOTBALL GAME THIS WEEKEND.

REALLY?

YEAH, I THINK IT'S AWESOME THAT YOU STUCK IT OUT AND NOW YOU'RE GOING TO THE CHAMPIONSHIP.

THANKS...

HUH. A COUPLE WEEKS AGO, SHE'D SAID IT WAS WEIRD, BUT I DIDN'T FEEL LIKE FIGHTING.

YEAH... WELL, GOOD LUCK. I'LL SEE YA THERE.

OKAY.

SEE YA.

I WANTED TO FORGIVE HER.

I WANTED TO BE FRIENDS AGAIN, BUT THINGS WERE DIFFERENT NOW. **WE** WERE DIFFERENT.

THE CHAMPIONSHIP GAME WAS **FINALLY** HERE.

WITH ALL THE EXCITEMENT, NO ONE SEEMED TO EVEN NOTICE THE COLD. FAMILIES AND FRIENDS HELD UP SIGNS IN THE STANDS AS THEY CHEERED FOR THEIR TEAM AND STOMPED THEIR FEET ON THE METAL BLEACHERS, CREATING A SOUND SO LOUD, I WAS SURPRISED THE WHOLE GROUND WASN'T SHAKING.

IT WAS PRETTY SURREAL.

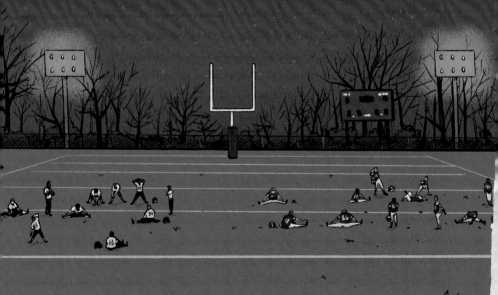

BRING IT IN, BEARS!

CAMPFIELD HAS ONLY LOST **ONE** GAME.

ONE. GAME.

THIS ISN'T GOING TO BE EASY.

YOU'RE GOING TO HAVE TO PLAY HARDER THAN YOU'VE EVER PLAYED BEFORE.

BUT I BELIEVE IN US.

ARE YOU READY?

YES, COACH!

ARE YOU READY?!

YES, COACH!

GOOD. BECAUSE IT'S GAME TIME!

SURPRISINGLY, I WASN'T NERVOUS. I WAS JUST PUMPED AND READY TO WIN.

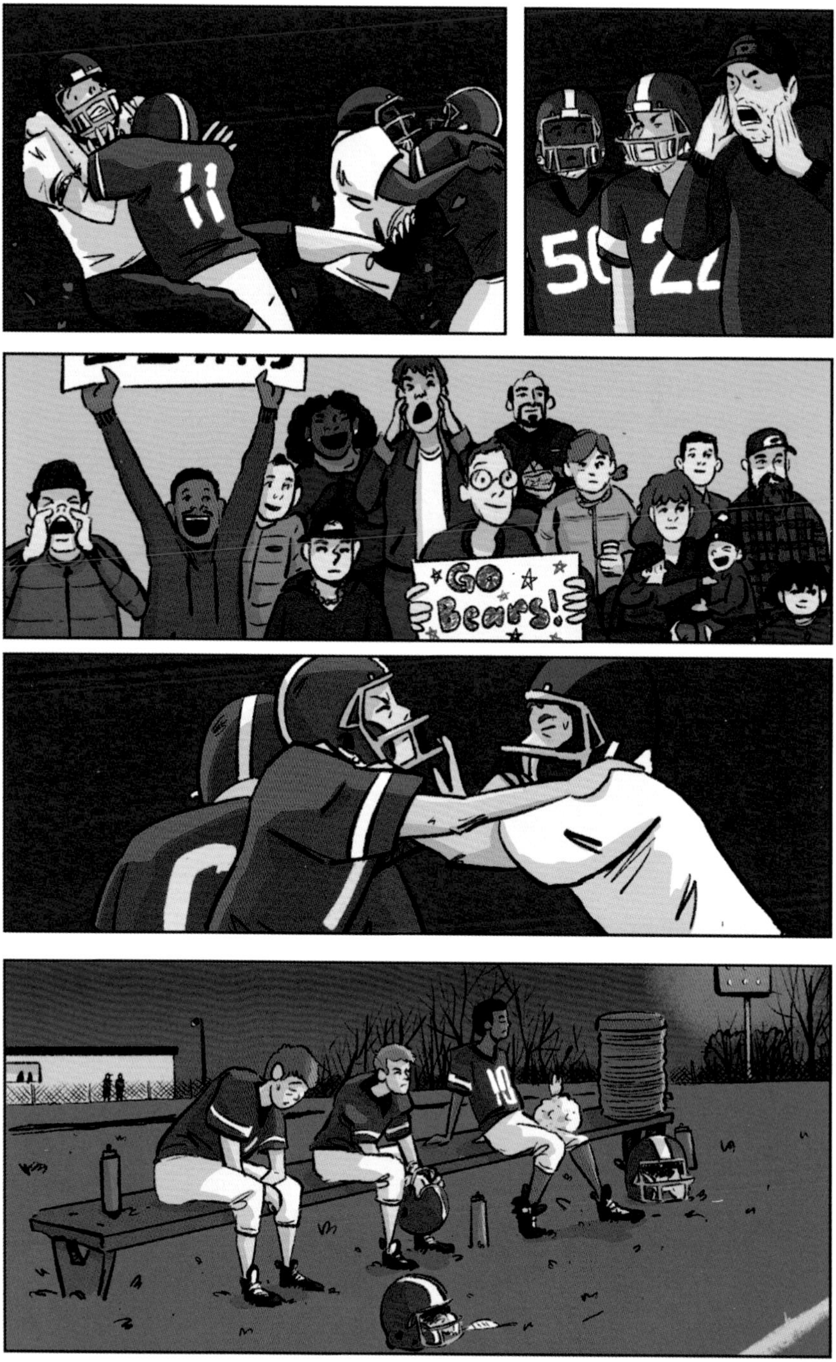
Go Bears!

HOME 03:41 VISITOR

00 00

3 DOWN 08 TO GO ON 38 QTR 3

THIS GAME WAS BY FAR THE MOST CHALLENGING YET.

I WAS PUSHING MYSELF BEYOND WHAT I'D EVER THOUGHT I WAS CAPABLE OF.

I WAS EXHAUSTED. READY TO COLLAPSE.

BUT THEN...

HIKE!

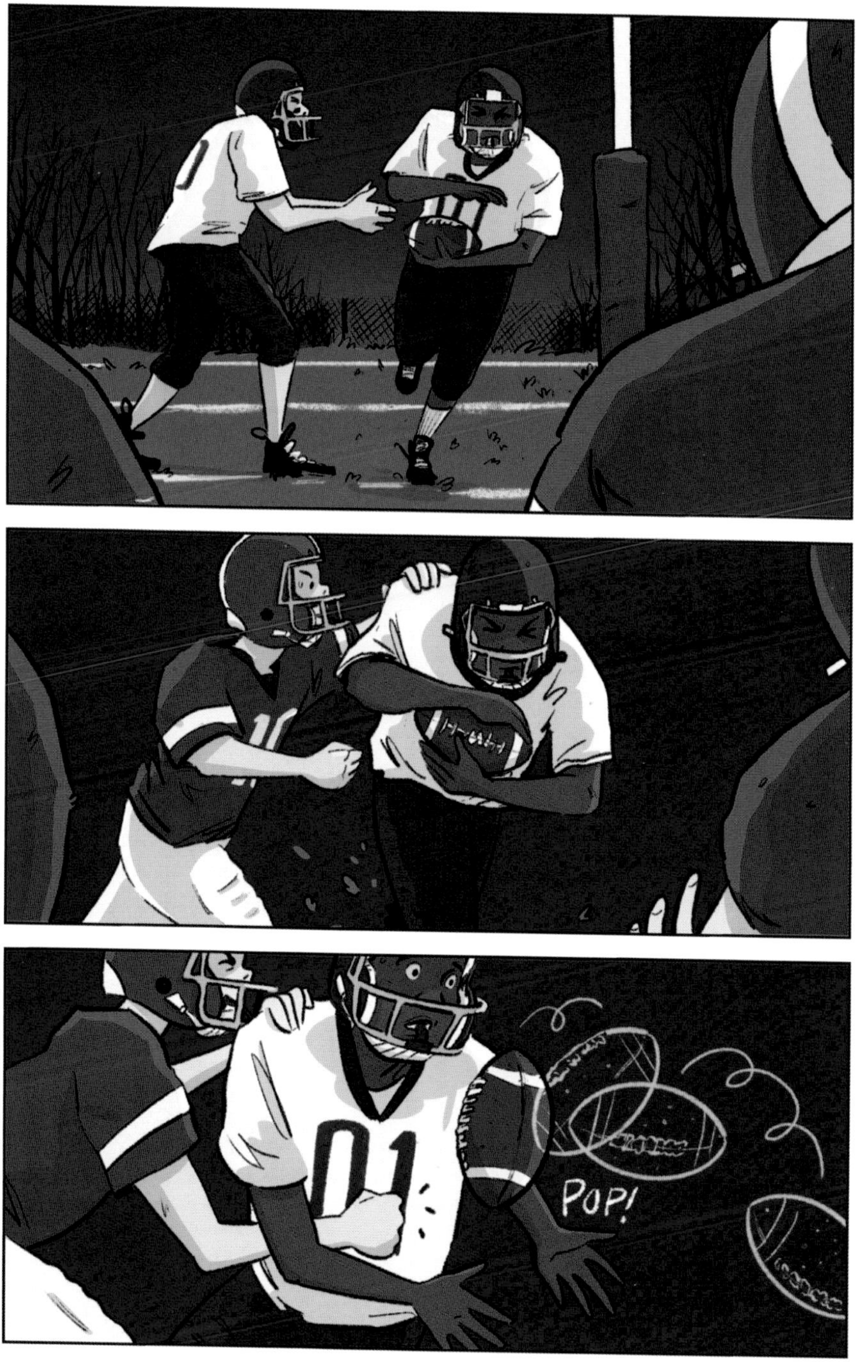
POP!

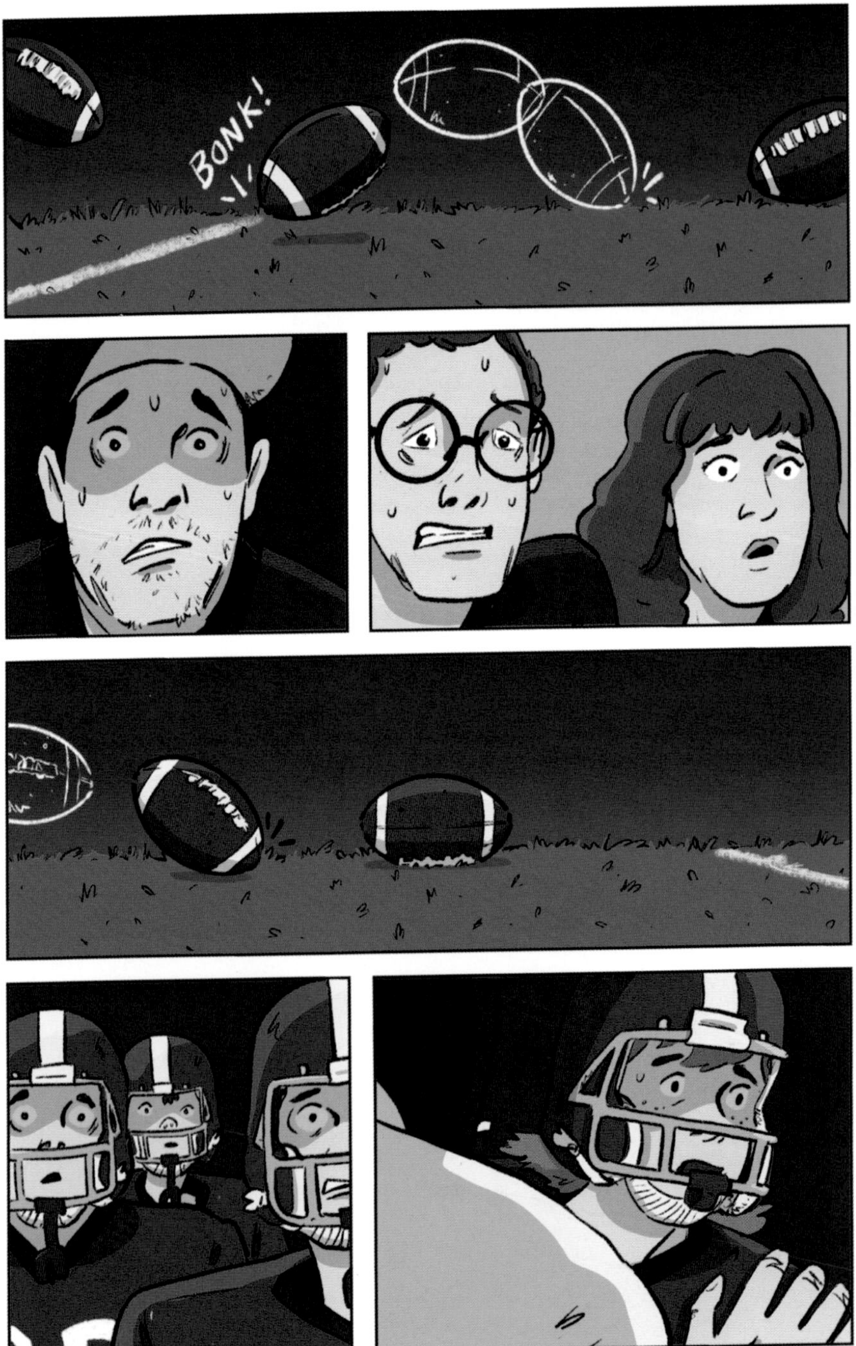
BONK!

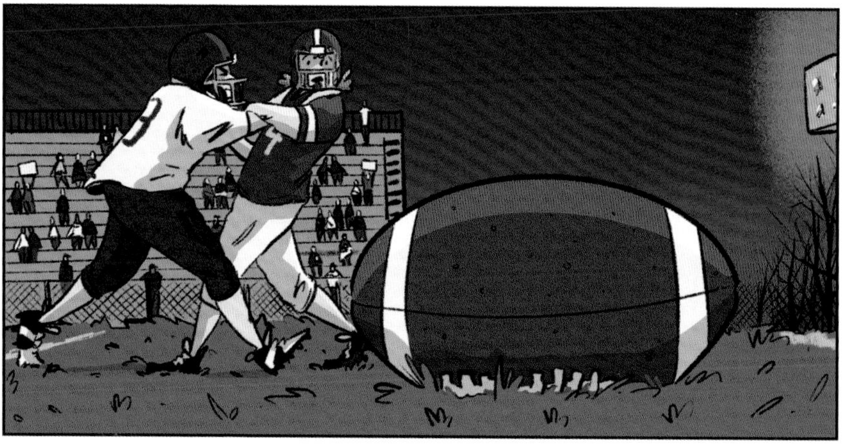

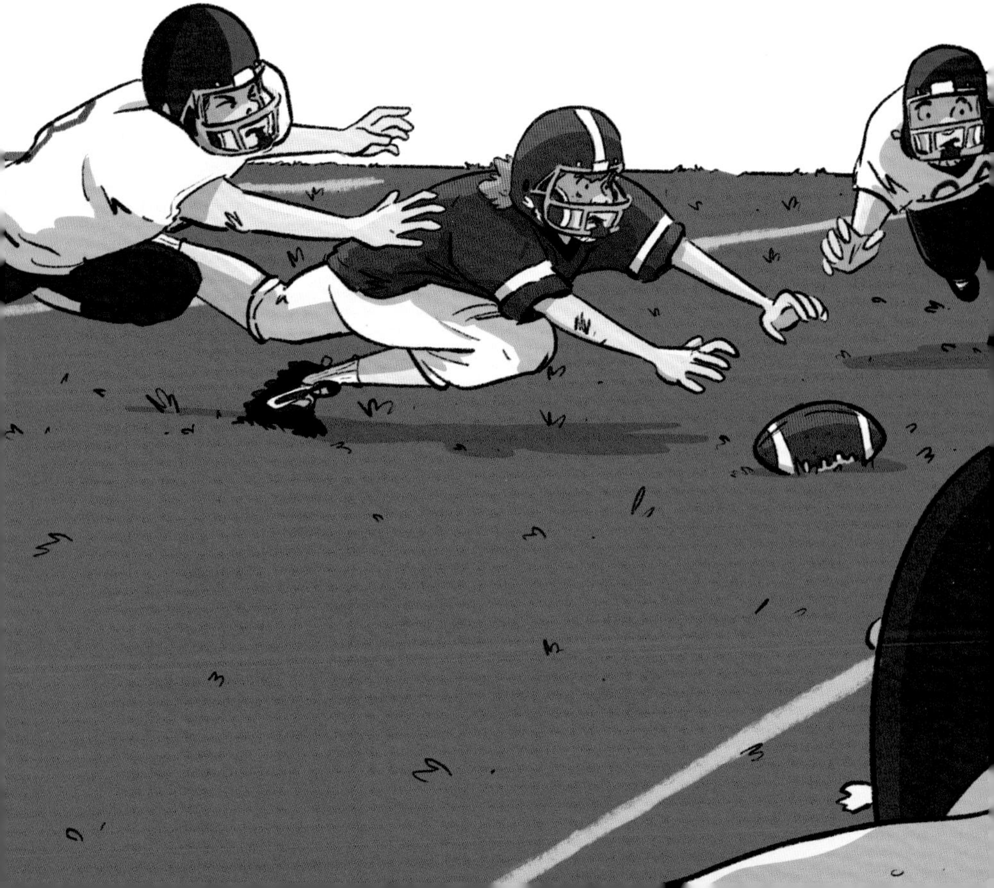

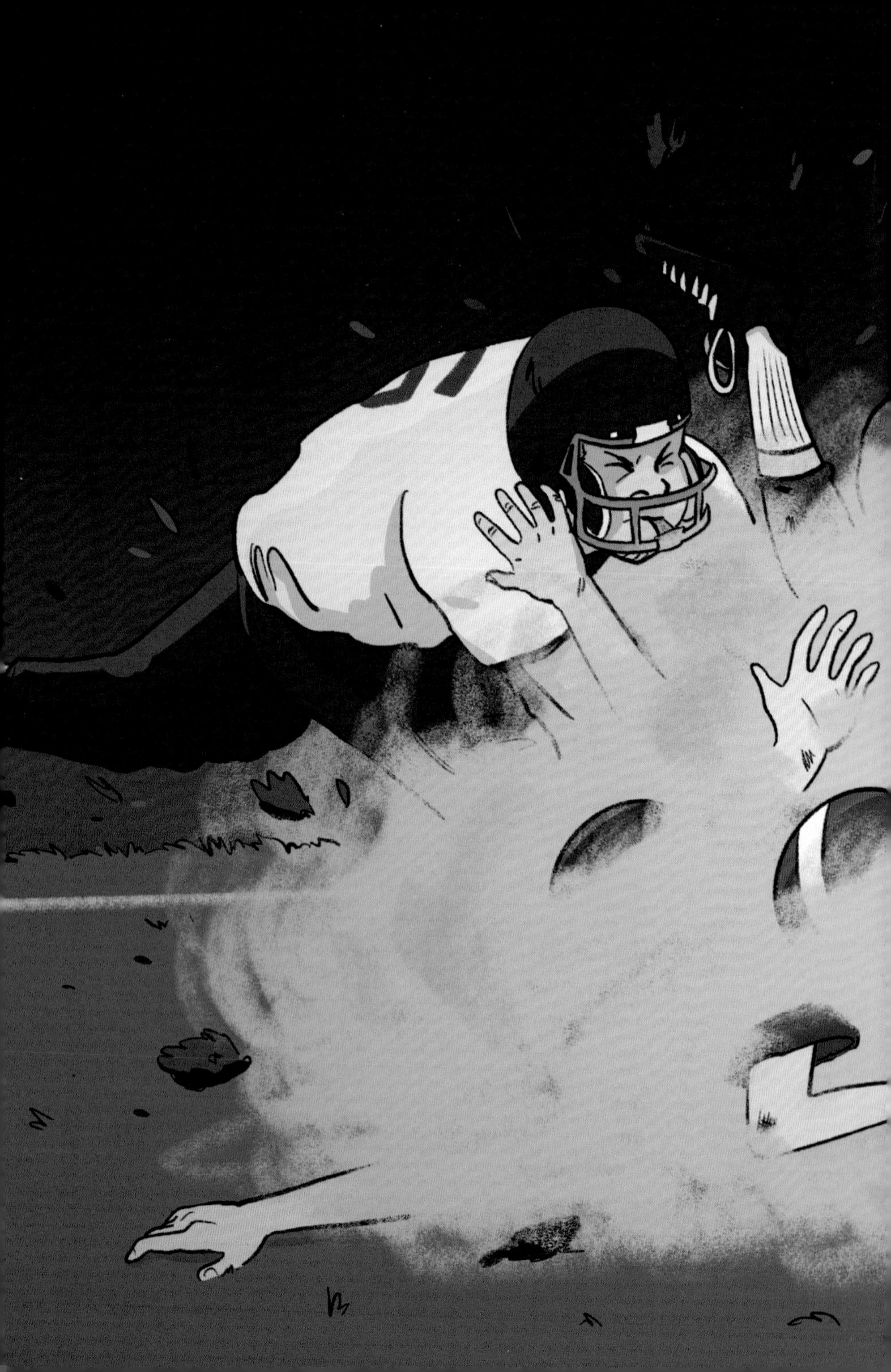

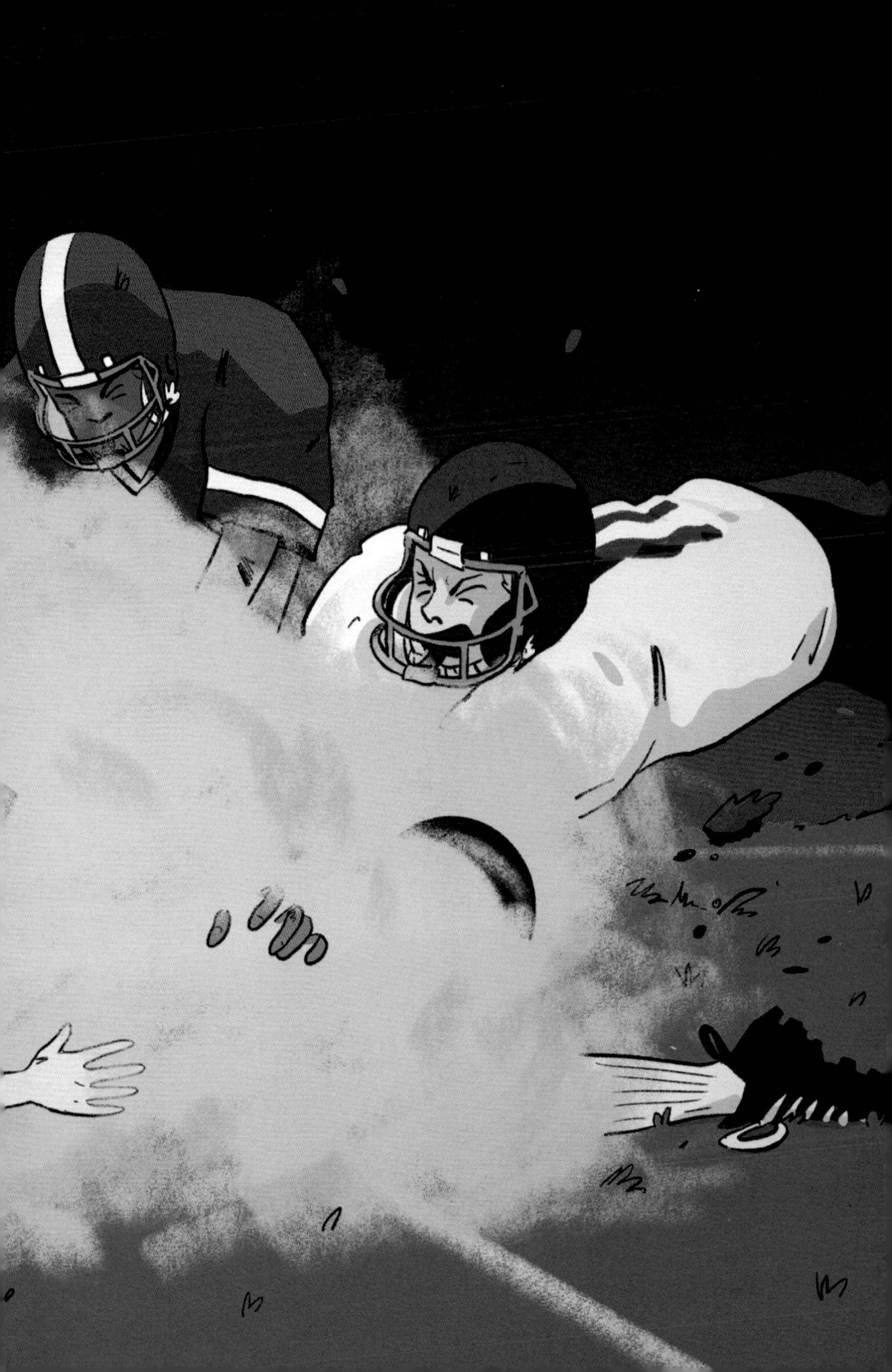

CRASH

BANG

SLAM

I BLEW THE WHISTLE!

THE PLAY'S OVER! **GET OFF!**

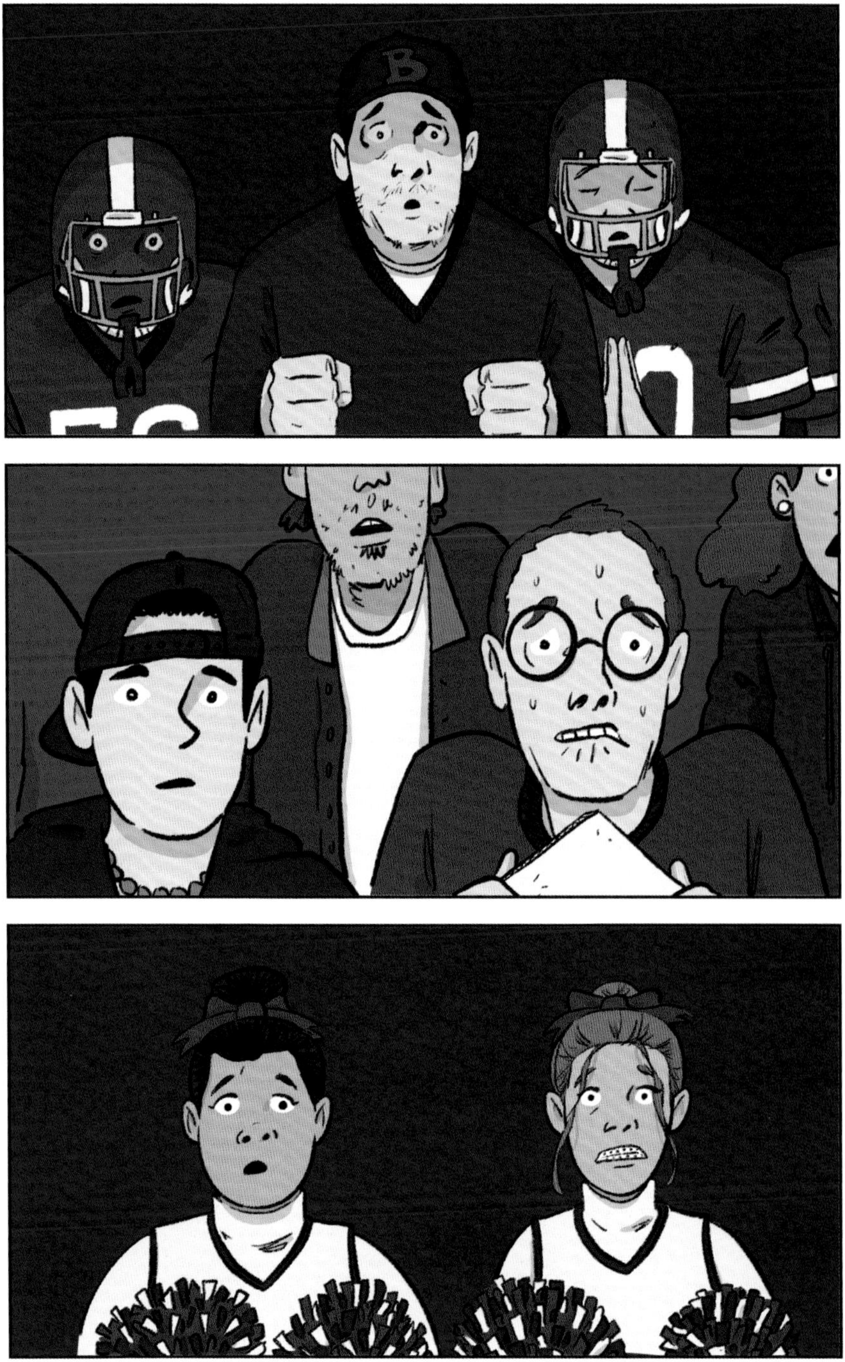

I COULDN'T BELIEVE I RECOVERED A FUMBLE!

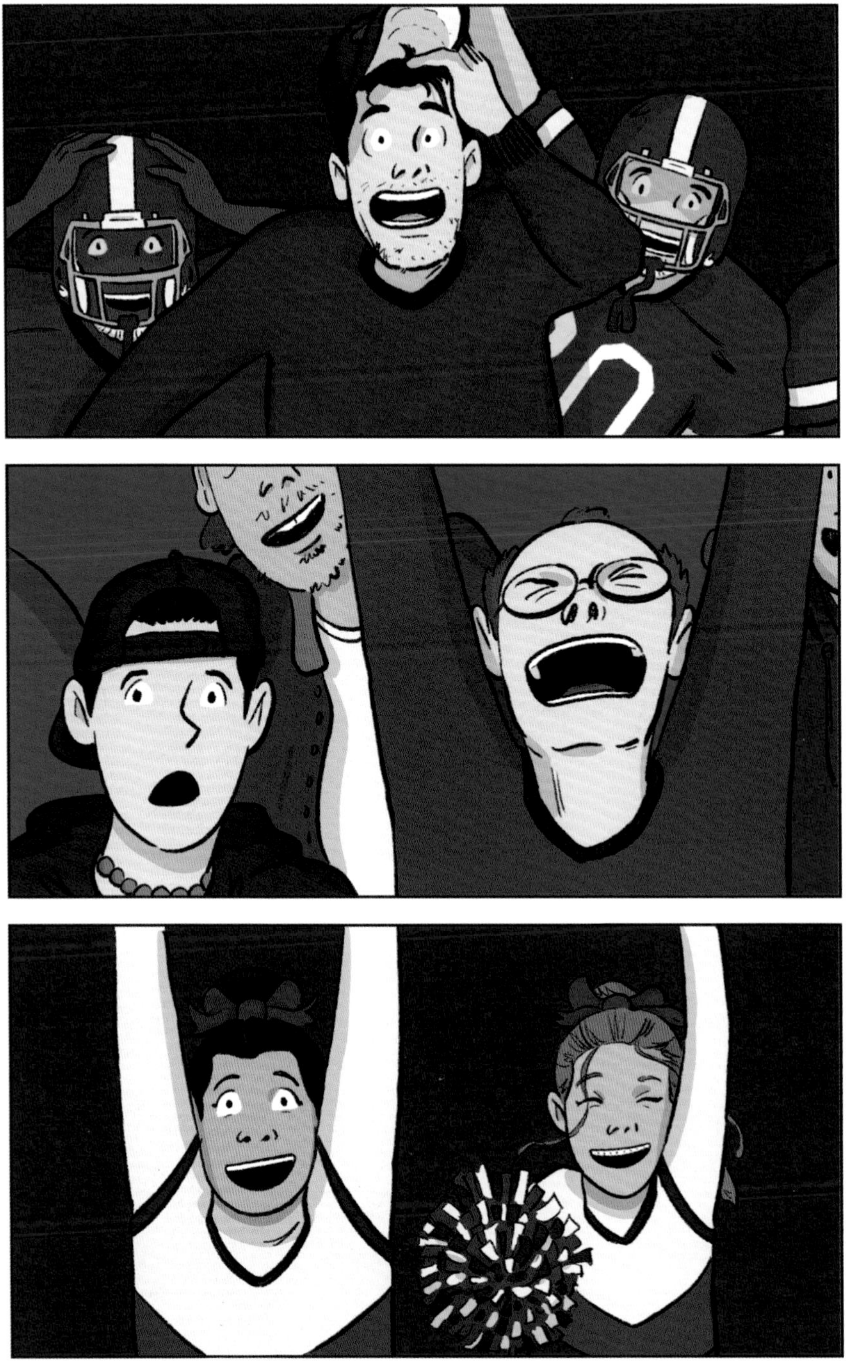

LATER.

HOME 00 · 00:35 · VISITOR 00

2 DOWN · 10 TO GO ON · 5 QTR · 4

MISTY, GET BACK IN THERE ON DEFENSE.

10:35

THE GAME WAS **INTENSE**, WITH NEITHER TEAM ABLE TO SCORE. IT WOULD TAKE A MIRACLE IN THE LAST THIRTY-FIVE SECONDS IF WE WERE GONNA SOMEHOW GET POSSESSION OF THE BALL **AND** SCORE.

HIKE!

I **NEEDED** TO GET TO THEIR QUARTERBACK. IT WAS PROBABLY OUR ONLY HOPE.

INSTEAD, I FELL ON TOP OF THE OFFENSIVE PLAYER BLOCKING ME...

...LEAVING AN OPENING FOR BEN TO GET THROUGH.

UH-OH...

CRACK!

SAFETY!

A SAFETY HAPPENS WHEN THE PLAYER CARRYING THE BALL IS TACKLED IN THEIR OWN END ZONE. THIS IS VERY RARE IN A FOOTBALL GAME. THE DEFENSIVE TEAM GETS TWO POINTS **AND** THE BALL!

WE WERE WINNING WITH ONLY SIX SECONDS LEFT IN THE GAME.

ALL WE HAD TO DO NOW WAS RUN OUT THE CLOCK.

THAT'S THE GAME! **BEARS WIN!**

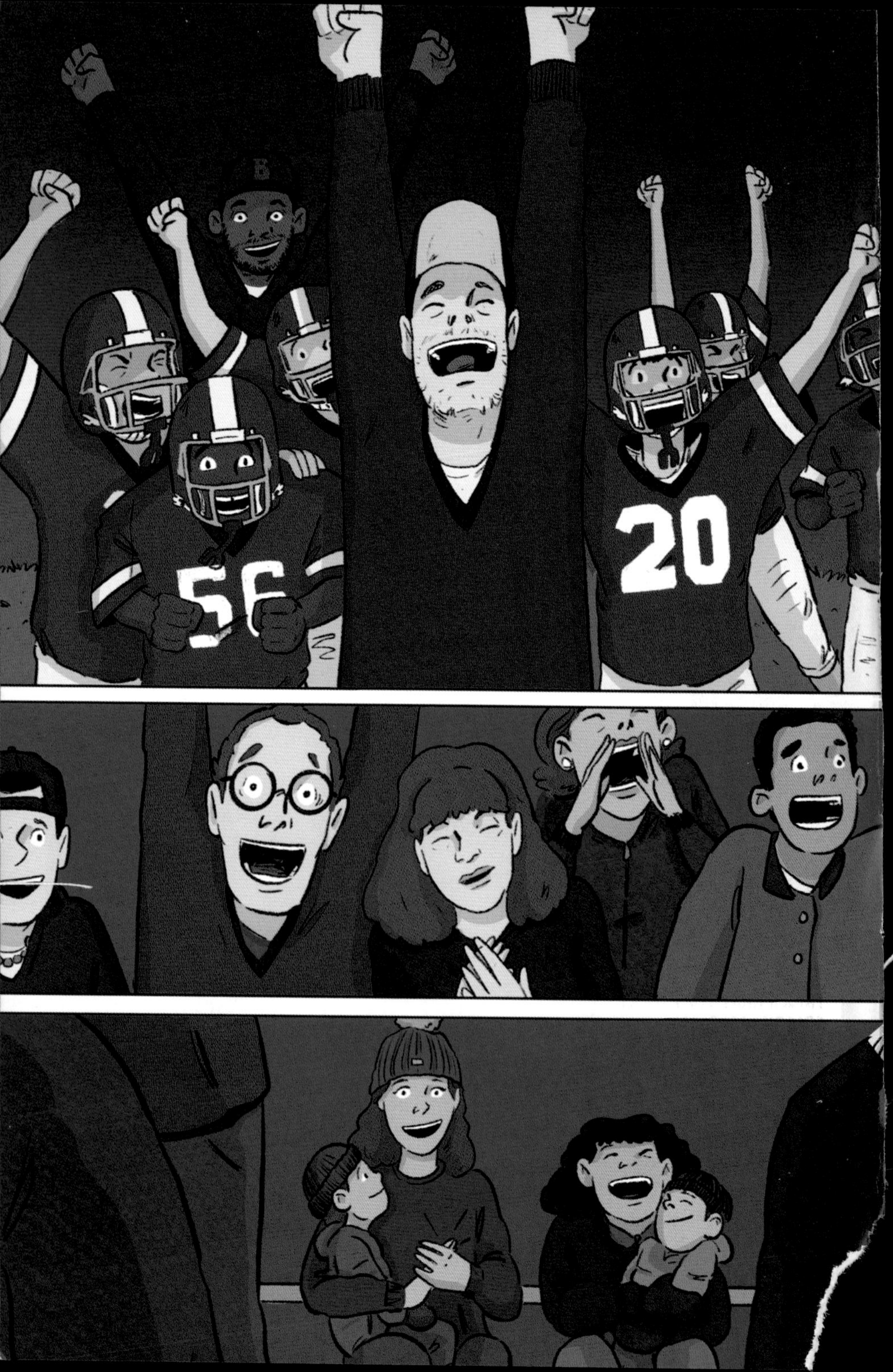
56
20

I NEEDED SOMEONE TO PINCH ME. I **HAD** TO BE DREAMING!

AND EVEN IN OUR MOST TRIUMPHANT MOMENT OF THE SEASON, COLE CONTINUED TO BE A JERK TO ME.

IT WAS TIME TO FACE IT: NOT EVERYONE WAS GONNA ACCEPT ME.

MISTY!

CONGRATULATIONS!

WHAT'S WRONG?

I'M JUST SO...

...HAPPY!

AND SO SAD IT'S OVER!

YOU'RE A CHAMPION!

WE ARE SO PROUD OF YOU!

HEY.

MY DAD IS HERE TO PICK ME UP, BUT I JUST WANTED TO SAY CONGRATULATIONS.

THANKS.

I'M REALLY SORRY I WAS SO MEAN.

CALL ME IF YOU WANT TO SPEND THE NIGHT SOON.

OKAY, BYE.

44

44

56

MAYBE IT WASN'T THE PERFECT APOLOGY, BUT IT GAVE ME A LITTLE HOPE THAT MAYBE WE'D BE FRIENDS AGAIN... SOMEDAY.

AWESOME GAME!

WE DID IT. A PERFECT SEASON.

YEAH, I'M STILL IN SHOCK!

WE'RE ALL GOING TO GET ICE CREAM IF YOU WANT TO COME. ALL THE CHEERLEADERS CAN COME, TOO.

OKAY. THANKS!

ICE CREAM?

I'LL COME, BUT I DON'T THINK I'LL **EVER** BE ABLE TO EAT ICE CREAM AGAIN IN MY LIFE.

SAME.

HA-HA!

MIDDLE SCHOOL WAS COMPLICATED.

BUT I KNEW ONE THING FOR SURE: I WAS **DONE** TRYING TO BE SOMEONE ELSE.

I WASN'T ANY GOOD AT IT, ANYWAY.

CONE-GRATULATIONS, EVERYBODY!

AY-YI-YI...

HA!

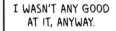

I FINALLY FOUND EXACTLY WHERE I FIT IN...
...WITH PEOPLE WHO DIDN'T CARE IF I STOOD OUT—OR THAT I MIGHT BE A LITTLE WEIRD.
AND WITH THEM BY MY SIDE, I WAS READY FOR MY NEXT ADVENTURE...
I WAS THINKING MAYBE SHOW CHOIR. I MEAN, I DID HAVE SOME PRETTY AWESOME DANCE MOVES.

AUTHOR'S NOTE

While this is the true story of my football season in seventh grade, recalling details from decades ago can be difficult. I did my best to faithfully depict what I remember about events and people at that time—especially myself. I used my diaries from middle school and interviewed family members as part of my research.

In most cases, names and likenesses were changed to protect the privacy of the real-life people represented in this book—most of whom I no longer have relationships with. In addition, certain characters and storylines were consolidated, and in a few cases, somewhat fictionalized for the purpose of streamlining the story.

SOME FUN FACTS:

• I NEVER TOLD "CHARLIE" I LIKED HIM. I WAS WAY TOO SHY! BY THE FOLLOWING SUMMER, THOUGH, I HAD A CRUSH ON HIS COUSIN.

• I DIDN'T PLAY FOOTBALL AGAIN AFTER SEVENTH GRADE. BY EIGHTH GRADE, THE BOYS WERE BIGGER THAN ME, AS CRAIG HAD PREDICTED, AND I WORRIED I WOULDN'T BE AS GOOD AS THEM ANYMORE. NOW I REALLY WISH I'D AT LEAST TRIED.

IMPORTANT NOTE: In 2019, the Surgeon General of the United States released a warning that tackle football is dangerous for children because of repeated hits to the head. If you are interested in playing, please talk with an adult and research the most up-to-date information. Note: Flag football is a fun alternative, and it's also super awesome!

ACKNOWLEDGMENTS

Thank you to my brilliant editor, Donna Bray, for believing in this book, for being patient through approximately one million revisions, and for helping me to shape it into what it is today. I don't even have the words to express how grateful I am to have you as an editor. Thank you to my agent, Daniel Lazar, for making all of this possible, for your guidance and support, and for helping me believe I can do this whole writing thing. Thank you to Torie Doherty-Munro for always answering our questions and for everything you do behind the scenes. Thank you to Dana Fritts, Laura Harshberger, and Tiara Kittrell, for working your magic to help bring this book into the world. Thank you to David Wilson—my husband, the illustrator of this book, and the most selfless person I know—for being able to read my mind and completely understand and capture twelve-year-old Misty, for cheering me on when I doubted myself, and for helping me write this book for nearly two whole years. Thank you for supporting me in everything I do—and for giving me the time to do it (aka watching the kids). Thank you to early readers Jay Wilson and Chad Lewis for

the feedback. Thank you to my family, especially my mom and stepdad, for always supporting me in my endeavors, no matter how wild they seem. Thank you to my writer friends for helping me navigate publishing, for answering my questions, giving feedback, listening to me vent, letting me bounce ideas off of you, and for being an all-around wonderful support system: Jess Burkhart, Jessica James, Jennifer Iacopelli, Erica Davis (especially for the jokes!), Isabel Sterling, Shelly Page, Vanessa Montalban, and the #22debuts Slack group. Thank you to all of my students at Walls and Crestwood Intermediate School for inspiring me to write my story and for your excitement throughout the publishing process. Thank you to my seventh-grade football coaches for never treating me any differently than the boys on the team. And lastly, thank you to *Julie and the Phantoms*, my comfort show that played on repeat when writing was just plain hard (and when it wasn't), and to AO3 for being a bright spot in a tough year and for making me a better writer.

—MISTY

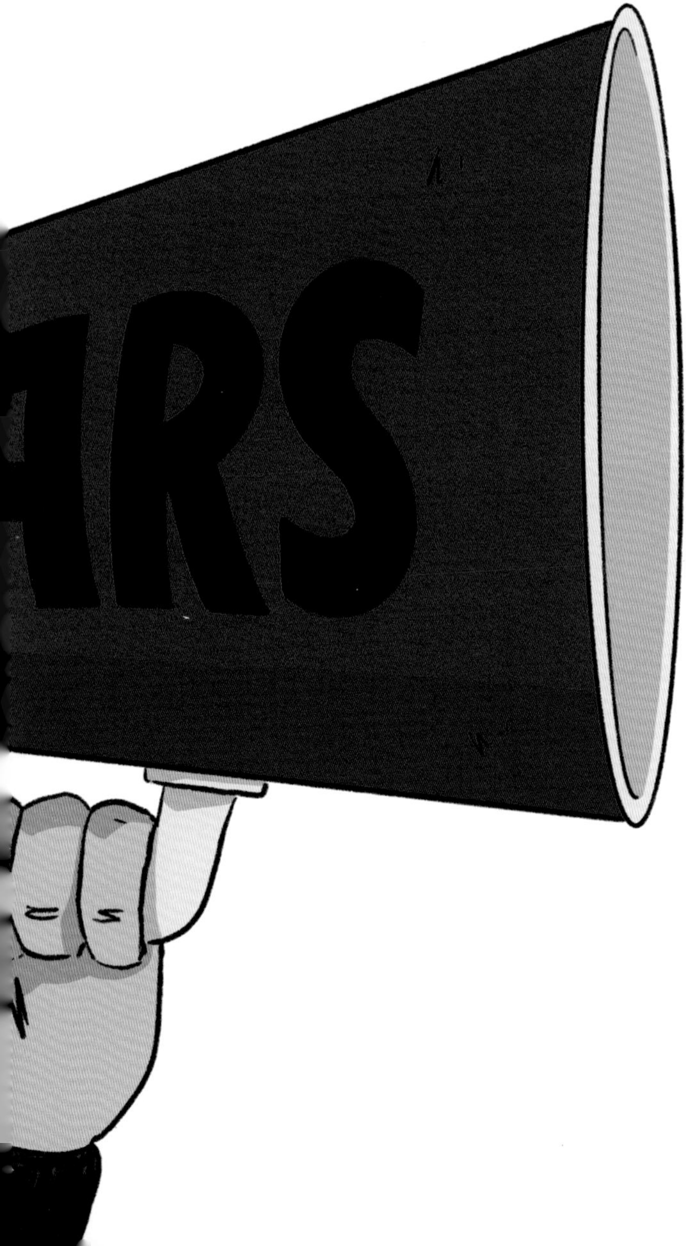
ARS

Thank you to editor extraordinaire, Donna Bray, for your confidence and insight. Daniel Lazar for all your hard work and guidance along the way. Dana Fritts for your expertise. Mom and Dad, for all the support. The Wilson brothers and the Air Dave Sunday football league. Matt Stansberry and Chad Lewis, my creative partners in crime. Dustin Dolerhie and Kevin Beers for being there when I needed to escape the creative side for a moment. Anne Trubek, for your wisdom and friendship. Ken Visocky O'Grady, for your enthusiasm and understanding. Jerry Kalback, for helping me become the illustrator I am today. Misty, you never cease to amaze me. And it seems as if you haven't changed much since middle school Misty—jumping into whatever your heart desires. Whether it's hospitality management, nursing, teaching, raising kids, playing football, or writing books. You are a great example of someone who proves that anything is possible if you put your mind to it. Thank you for sharing your journey with me.

—DAVID